"I DON'T SOUND LIKE NOBODY."

"What kind of singer are you?" she asked.

"I sing all kinds," Elvis said.

"Who do you sound like?"

"I don't sound like nobody."

"What do you sing? Hillbilly?"

"I sing hillbilly."

"Well, who do you sound like in hillbilly?"

"I don't sound like nobody."

Finally, the studio was ready, and Elvis went in with his guitar and began to sing the main song he had come to record—"My Happiness." It was a ballad he had sung many times on the steps at the Courts, for his mom and her friends, and for the girls. For the flip side he sang "That's When Your Heartaches Begin." Years later, Elvis recalled that his guitar playing "sounded like somebody beating on a bucket lid."

Marion had listened in while Elvis made his record, and from the first plaintive, quavering notes he sang, she realized he was right. He didn't sound like anybody else.

READ ALL THE BOOKS IN THE UP*close* SERIES

Up Close: Johnny Cash	Anne E. Neimark
Up Close: Robert F. Kennedy	Marc Aronson
Up Close: Elvis Presley	Wilborn Hampton
Up Close: Oprah Winfrey	Ilene Cooper
Up Close: Frank Lloyd Wright	Jan Adkins

ELVIS PRESLEY

a twentieth-century life by

WILBORN HAMPTON

PUFFIN BOOKS

For Douglas
This was how your Dad learned to rock and roll

PUFFIN BOOKS
Published by the Penguin Group
Penguin Young Readers Group, 345 Hudson Street, New York, New York 10014, U.S.A.
Penguin Group (Canada), 90 Eglinton Avenue East, Suite 700, Toronto, Ontario, Canada M4P 2Y3
(a division of Pearson Penguin Canada Inc.)
Penguin Books Ltd, 80 Strand, London WC2R 0RL, England
Penguin Ireland, 25 St Stephen's Green, Dublin 2, Ireland (a division of Penguin Books Ltd)
Penguin Group (Australia), 250 Camberwell Road, Camberwell, Victoria 3124, Australia
(a division of Pearson Australia Group Pty Ltd)
Penguin Books India Pvt Ltd, 11 Community Centre, Panchsheel Park, New Delhi - 110 017, India
Penguin Group (NZ), 67 Apollo Drive, Rosedale, North Shore 0632, New Zealand
(a division of Pearson New Zealand Ltd)
Penguin Books (South Africa) (Pty) Ltd, 24 Sturdee Avenue,
Rosebank, Johannesburg 2196, South Africa

Registered Offices: Penguin Books Ltd, 80 Strand, London WC2R 0RL, England

First published in the United States of America by Viking,
a division of Penguin Young Readers Group, 2007
Published by Puffin Books, a division of Penguin Young Readers Group, 2008

1 3 5 7 9 10 8 6 4 2

Photo credits can be found on page 199.

LIBRARY OF CONGRESS CATALOGING-IN-PUBLICATION DATA
Hampton, Wilborn.
Elvis Presley, a twentieth century life / by Wilborn Hampton.
p. cm—(Up close)
ISBN 978-0-670-06166-2 (hardcover)
1. Presley, Elvis, 1935–1977—Juvenile literature.
2. Rock musicians—United States—Biography—Juvenile literature.
[1. Presley, Elvis, 1935–1977. 2. Singers.] I. Title. II. Title: Elvis Presley, a 20th century life.
ML3930.P73H35 2007
782.42166092—dc22 [B] 2006029074

Printed in the U.S.A.
Set in Goudy
Book design by Jim Hoover

Puffin Books ISBN 978-0-14-241148-3

CONTENTS

ELVIS PRESLEY

FOREWORD

THE FIRST TIME I heard Elvis Presley was in the fall of 1954. I was in my final year of junior high school. It was a Saturday, and I had gone roller skating with a couple of friends. We had rented our skates and were gliding around the rink to the usual dance music, checking out the girls, when a new song burst over the sound system.

It made me want to shout out loud. It was like nothing I had ever heard. I knew and liked Bill Haley's "Rock Around the Clock," regarded by some as the first rock-and-roll song, but this was something else. This was a cry from the heart, a rebel yell announcing the advent of a new music. The girls were momentarily forgotten and I started trying to skate to the upbeat tempo of the song. I think I fell down. It's not easy to rock and roll on roller skates.

As soon as the song was over, I skated over to the disc jockey and asked him what the song was. It was a record he had just gotten in and he had to look at the label. He said it was called "Good Rockin' Tonight." Who was the singer? He looked at the label again. "Elvis Presley." I asked him if he would play it again, and he did.

The next week I went to my local record store and asked for the record. The clerk seemed never to have heard of either the song or Elvis Presley. The following week I went downtown to the one record store in Dallas that might have it. It was a well-known store called the Record Mart and it was located in a section of town called "Deep Elm," which in the still-segregated society of the 1950s was a predominantly black area. It was not that it was a rough part of town, but, as in Beale Street in Memphis, the famous home of the blues, the presence of a white kid could draw stares.

The Record Mart had a copy and I bought it. The clerk there told me that it was actually Presley's second record, but they were out of the first one, a song called "That's All Right, Mama," and were waiting to get a new shipment in. I took my record home and played it over and over. Elvis had a new convert to rock and roll.

Another early memory of Elvis is from a couple of years later. It was summer and several of the neighborhood kids were in the backyard of a family that had three daughters. We had a record player, and somebody put on a copy of "Heartbreak Hotel," Elvis's first new record for the RCA label. We all jumped up and started bopping around on the grass.

Suddenly the back door of the house next door opened. The woman who lived there, who was known as a sort of religious fanatic, stepped outside and began to scream at us: "Jezebels! You should all be ashamed of yourselves. That music is evil." She went on for a few minutes.

We had stopped in our tracks when she started her tirade, and when she finally ran out of steam and went back inside, we turned the volume down and went on dancing.

Elvis's story is at once both heartwarming and heartbreaking. It is the story of a poor boy from the wrong side of the tracks who became a king, an outsider who pursued his dream despite the ridicule and derision of his peers. It is also a cautionary tale of the dangers of excess and the corruption of fame.

Whether you loved him or hated him, Elvis left no one indifferent to rock and roll. And whether for good or ill, he almost single-handedly changed the musical culture not only of America but of the world. As John Lennon of the Beatles once said, "Before there was Elvis, there was nothing."

At every stop on his 1955 tour, crowds of screaming fans, mostly girls, mobbed Elvis.

INTRODUCTION

IN MAY 1955, Elvis Presley was appearing as one of the acts on Colonel Thomas A. Parker's traveling country western show, playing twenty cities in three weeks. The show was headlined by top country recording artists like Hank Snow, Slim Whitman, and the Carter Sisters with Mother Maybelle.

Elvis was then a twenty-year-old singer who in less than a year had had four singles issued by Sun Records, a little-known label run by Sam Phillips in Memphis. From the first engagement, on May 1 in New Orleans, Elvis's appearances had been generating a lot of excitement, especially among young girls in the audience, all of whom seemed to go into throes of ecstasy for the singer who had a habit of shaking his leg and swiveling his hips when he performed.

By the time the tour reached Florida, everybody was talking about the reception Elvis was getting from the girls, and Colonel Parker's publicist in the Sunshine State, Mae Axton, decided to interview Elvis for the tour's publicity packet. As she recalled later for Peter Guralnick, Elvis's biographer, she asked him about his gyrations onstage:

> Mae: You know, what I can't understand is how you keep that leg shaking just at the right tempo all the time you're singing.
>
> Elvis: Well, it gets hard sometimes. I have to stop and rest it—but it just automatically wiggles like that.
>
> Mae: Is that it? Just automatically does it?
>
> Elvis: Yes, ma'am.

The tour's first stop in Florida was Daytona Beach, and Mae remembered coming across Elvis standing outside their motel and staring at the Atlantic. Elvis had never seen the ocean, and he turned to her and said: "Mrs. Axton, look at that ocean. I can't believe it's so big. I'd give anything in the world to find enough money to bring my mother and daddy down here to see it."

Mae, who was a high school English teacher when she wasn't moonlighting for the Colonel, took an instant liking to the boy who was so shy and polite offstage and, by all accounts, so full of explosive energy onstage. That night she went to see him perform for the first time. She saw a former student in the audience with some other girls, and they were all jumping up and down and squealing. After Elvis finished, Mae went up to the girl and asked her, "Honey, what is it about this kid?" The girl smiled sheepishly and replied, "Awww, Mrs. Axton, he's just a great big beautiful hunk of forbidden fruit."

If Elvis's music and delivery were not exactly in the country western mold, his dress set him apart even more. Instead of the cowboy shirts and hats that most of the other performers on the tour wore, Elvis came onstage in pink and black outfits—ruffled shirts with turned-up collars, and loud jackets.

On May 13, the tour was scheduled to play a concert before fourteen thousand people at the Gator Bowl in Jacksonville. Before the show, Elvis went to dinner with Mae and some of the other musicians. The women began to tease him about the frilly pink shirt he was wearing. Mae told him he should give the shirt to her because it would make a pretty blouse. June Carter said no, he should give the shirt to her. Another woman at the table said she wanted it. Then Mae said, "Elvis, you should give it to one of us because they're just going to tear it off you tonight." Elvis laughed.

Elvis by now had moved up to the last act on the first half of the show, just before intermission. At the end of his performance, Elvis leaned into the microphone and said, "Girls, I'll see you all backstage."

It was like an open invitation. No sooner had Elvis left the stage than maybe a hundred girls from the audience charged after him, their footsteps thundering down the ramp toward the football stadium's dressing rooms. Elvis started running. Four policemen who were there to provide security chased after them.

Mae was in an adjacent office counting the receipts from the show with Colonel Parker. She heard all the commotion and went out to see what was happening. The Colonel and some musicians who were backstage followed her. When they got to the locker room, they saw Elvis on top of one of the showers, with the girls, some of whom had climbed through a window, grabbing at him. Elvis looked scared. His shirt had been ripped to shreds and so had his coat. He didn't even have his belt or his shoes and socks. All he had on was his pants, and the girls were trying to get at those.

The policemen started pulling the girls out of the locker room, and eventually Elvis climbed down from the shower. By the next day, when the press picked up on the story, Elvis Presley was not only front-page news but a national phenomenon that embodied what came to be known as rock and roll.

CHAPTER ONE

WHEN HE WAS ten years old, Elvis Presley was hoping that his parents would give him a bicycle for his next birthday, and he made no secret about it. Most of the other kids he knew had bikes, and Elvis wanted one, too. But times were hard for the Presley family in that winter of 1945–46, following the end of World War II. So instead of a bicycle, his parents gave Elvis a little guitar.

It seems incredible to contemplate now, but the future of American culture may have changed forever because of a birthday present to a boy in Tupelo, Mississippi.

The gift of the guitar, of course, was not the beginning of young Elvis Presley's interest in music. Like so many other musicians who came out of the Depression and World War II eras, his first exposure to music came from church, and throughout his youth the music that captivated him most was gospel.

During his childhood, Elvis's parents attended the First Assembly of God church in East Tupelo. It was where his parents had met, and they continued to attend regularly after they eloped in 1933. The Assembly of God is a Pentecostal church that some people disparagingly refer to as a "holy-roller" church because of the uninhibited nature of its worship services, in which music plays a big part.

Unlike most other Protestant denominations that are content with an organ or piano to accompany their choirs, the Assembly of God uses all kinds of musical instruments—brass, winds, banjos, drums, and guitars—just about anything that can be used to fulfill the commandment to "make a joyful noise to the Lord."

The music at church spoke to Elvis's soul from the start, and when he was only two years old, he would climb down from his mother's lap and race up the aisle to join the church choir, dancing up and down and trying to sing along with them.

* * *

Elvis Aron Presley was born on January 8, 1935, at about four o'clock in the morning, to Gladys and Vernon Presley, in a two-room house in East Tupelo, Mississippi, that his father had built with the help of his grandfather and uncle. There was no bathroom, running water, or electricity. It had an outhouse at the back, a pump, and oil lamps for lighting. His parents had moved into the house just a month before he was born.

Elvis was one of twins who were delivered to Gladys that morning. His brother, given the name Jesse Garon, was stillborn about half an hour before Elvis was born. Throughout his life, Elvis would sometimes mention his brother, and as a boy he often visited his grave in Priceville Cemetery. After the delivery, both Gladys and Elvis were taken to a hospital, and his mother was unable to have another child.

When Gladys Smith met Vernon Presley, the East Tupelo First Assembly of God church held services in a tent on a vacant lot. Gladys was four years older than Vernon, and when they married in June 1933, each lied on the application about their age. Vernon, who at seventeen was underage, said he was twenty-two; Gladys, who was twenty-one, said she was only nineteen. They had to borrow the three dollars for a marriage license from friends.

Gladys was the more outgoing of the two. A solidly built woman with a round face and a warm smile, Gladys was lively and talkative. She also had a steady job at the Tupelo Garment Plant. Vernon, square-shouldered and tall, had a brooding look and was more introverted, with little to say. He also had trouble keeping regular work.

In one way, however, Gladys and Vernon were the same. Each adored their son Elvis, although they showed it in different ways. Whatever hardships his childhood brought him, Elvis grew up as a much-loved boy. Two other factors were constants in the Presley household and would have a lasting influence on Elvis: music and money.

Elvis was born in the middle of what was known as the Great Depression, and the main concern for most American families during that period was just to pay the rent and put food on the table. This was a time before welfare or unemployment insurance. If you didn't have a job or a family to take you in, you went hungry and slept in the open.

The Presleys always had trouble making ends meet.

Gladys had quit her job when Elvis was born, and Vernon worked whenever he could—as a milkman, a handyman, a day laborer—but jobs were not that easy to find. In Vernon's scramble to support his family, he nearly lost them. Just before Elvis's third birthday, Vernon and his brother-in-law and another man were arrested and accused of forgery for altering a check for four dollars to make it appear it was for more money. Six months later the three men were sentenced to three years in prison.

Gladys and Elvis lived briefly with several different family members, and on weekends, Elvis and his mother would ride the bus to visit Vernon in jail. In the end, Vernon spent only eight months behind bars, but the episode had a lasting effect on the family and made Vernon even more reclusive than before.

The struggle for money haunted Elvis's childhood. Once when he heard his mother and father arguing about the bills, he came to his mother and told her: "Don't you worry. When I grow up, I'm going to buy you a fine house and pay everything you owe at the grocery store and get two Cadillacs—one for you and Daddy and one for me."

Later, after Elvis had fulfilled that promise beyond

Although his parents were poor, Elvis grew up a much loved child (circa 1938).

any of their wildest dreams, Vernon recalled the hard times they lived through. The family had never gone hungry, he said, but there were nights when all they had for supper was cornbread and water.

But if money was a constant worry in the Presley household, it could be forgotten for a time thanks to the music that was free over the radio and at church. Just as television would become a few years later, radio was the main source of entertainment for most Americans at that time, and nearly every family, no matter how poor, had one.

Besides the radio during the week and church services on Sunday, there were also outdoor concerts in Tupelo's Courthouse Square and in parks around town. Even at school, there were music programs in which students would play an instrument or sing. Elvis was surrounded by music, and it all soaked in. Gospel music remained his favorite as a child, but he listened to it all—hillbilly, country, blues. Elvis could hear a song two or three times and remember the words.

But for all of Elvis's love of music, it still surprised his parents when he got up on stage and sang before several hundred people at the Mississippi-Alabama Fair and Dairy Show in Tupelo. The appearance came about after Elvis, then in the fifth grade, sang "Old Shep," a well-known ballad about a boy and his dog, at a school program. His teacher, Mrs. Oleta Grimes, was so impressed she entered Elvis in a talent contest for children's day at the fair. Elvis was the only one who sang without accompaniment. All the other students had someone to play the guitar or piano for their performance. But Elvis just stood on a stool so he could reach the microphone and sang "Old Shep" a cappella.

This was just before his eleventh birthday, and the

fact that he was the only one to sing without any musical instrument may have given his parents the idea for their birthday gift. The guitar they gave him was not even a full-size one, but a smaller instrument, made for beginners. It could make music, however, for anyone who knew how to play it. But that was something Elvis still had to learn.

Just as the church ignited his love of music, it also provided him with his first guitar lessons. The pastor of the First Assembly of God church, Fred Smith, played the guitar at worship services. Elvis began to take his guitar by the church after school, and Smith would show him where to place his fingers to make the basic chords.

Soon, like Mary and her little lamb in the nursery rhyme, everywhere that Elvis went the guitar was sure to go. Elvis even started taking his guitar with him to school. Every day that it didn't rain, Elvis would walk to school with his guitar slung over his back and put it in his locker until lunch period, when he would take it out and go to the basement and strum it, trying out the new chords he had been taught.

The family moved often, but while they lived at various addresses in East Tupelo, Elvis continued to attend the consolidated school there that covered all grades from one through twelve. He was an average student, and he had friends, though not many. His natural shyness and the fact that Gladys walked with him to school led the other students to regard him as a "mama's boy."

In the summer before he entered the sixth grade, the Presleys moved from East Tupelo to Tupelo itself. It was a difficult experience for Elvis. He had to leave the few friends he had and enroll in a new school where he knew no one. From the start, he was regarded as an outsider by the other kids, not only because he often wore overalls to school but because he lived in a part of Tupelo, which was still racially segregated, that was considered "colored," as African Americans were politely called at the time.

In fact, his new neighborhood, known as Shake Rag, opened a window onto a world that would influence Elvis and expand his music in ways he would understand only much later. Shake Rag was crammed with black churches, black social clubs, and black schools, and the sounds of black music—blues, spirituals, and jazz—swept up and down its streets. There were revival meetings in vacant lots and dances in the social clubs. Elvis just breathed it all in. He stood on the outside, always the lone observer, but the music went straight to his soul.

Troubles at school, however, kept increasing. Shortly after Elvis started the eighth grade, some of the school's bullies grabbed his guitar and cut all the strings, as a prank against the hillbilly "white trash." Some of his friends chipped in and bought him another set.

A few weeks after that incident, Elvis's parents decided to move to Memphis. It is not clear exactly what persuaded Vernon and Gladys to leave Tupelo. Some people said it was because Vernon had been fired yet again. It almost certainly had to do with money. Memphis, about fifty miles north of Tupelo, was the big city where there was more opportunity for jobs.

Years later, Elvis recalled: "We were broke, man, broke. We left Tupelo overnight. . . . We just headed for Memphis. Things had to be better."

But in an interview Vernon gave shortly before he died, he suggested that the treatment Elvis was receiving at school might have been part of the reason. "Poor we were, I'll never deny that," Vernon said. "But trash we weren't. We never had any prejudice. We never put anybody down. Neither did Elvis."

CHAPTER TWO

FOR ELVIS, MEMPHIS was the gateway to his dreams. But simply moving to a new city doesn't automatically change one's life. At the start in Memphis, the Presleys still had money problems.

In September 1949, just over ten months after arriving in Memphis, Gladys and Vernon moved the family into a public housing project called Lauderdale Courts. The apartment they were assigned needed painting and had plumbing problems. But it had two bedrooms, a living room, a separate kitchen, and a bathroom. Elvis and his parents finally had a home.

Elvis enrolled in the ninth grade at Humes High School that fall and walked the ten blocks from the Courts to school every day. In the beginning, Gladys

In high school, Elvis grew sideburns and long hair, and began to create his own fashion style.

walked with him, but she soon stopped because the other students again teased him. In his freshman year, Elvis got Bs in English, science, and math. But he got a C in music, and his teacher told him the reason was that he couldn't sing. Elvis challenged her, saying he could sing, she just didn't appreciate his kind of singing. He brought his guitar to school the next day and sang "Keep Them Cold Icy Fingers Off of Me," a novelty hillbilly song. The teacher listened, then told him she agreed with him—she didn't appreciate his kind of singing.

Humes High was a large school, and Elvis went mostly unnoticed, although some of the older boys would make fun of him. But Elvis never seemed to let the taunting get to him.

At the Courts, however, Elvis made several friends with whom he would go to the movies, go swimming, or ride bikes. Some of them even formed a touch football team and played teams from other neighborhoods. In the summer after the ninth grade, Vernon bought Elvis a push lawnmower, and he and some other boys from the Courts would go around the neighborhood doing yard work at four dollars a lawn.

Throughout his first couple of years in Memphis, Elvis kept his abiding passion for music to himself. He never took his guitar to school, and he rarely carried it around the Courts. His friends knew he had a guitar and could play it a little, but it was not something Elvis made a big deal about.

But in Memphis, which had long been a mecca for the Negro blues and gospel music that grew out of the Southern cotton fields, Elvis was surrounded by music even more than he had been in Tupelo. Elvis attended either the Reverend J. J. Denson's Poplar Street Mission or the First Assembly of God to hear the singing, and he often went to the All-Night Gospel concerts on weekends at Ellis Auditorium.

And then there was the radio. Memphis in those days was awash in radio stations. Most of them were small with relatively weak transmitters that broadcast from hotels or storefront locations. Disc jockeys were not the celebrities many are today, and most of them had to hold down other jobs in addition to their radio shows.

One of the most popular in Memphis was a late-night show hosted by Dewey Phillips, known as

Daddy-O Dewey, that featured new music, a lot of it recorded at a studio run by Sam Phillips, a friend of but no relation to Daddy-O.

There were still a lot of live performances on the radio in those days, with studio audiences in attendance. B. B. King, for example, was a DJ who would play his own music live on the air over WDIA, a station that billed itself as "The Mother Station of the Negroes" because of its all-black programming. On Saturdays, Elvis sometimes went to the WMPS studio on the corner of Union and Main to watch the live broadcast of *High Noon Round-Up* with Bob Neal as the host, featuring live country performances.

Once again, however, it was through a connection at the church that he took the next step in his musical education. Although his parents had mostly stopped going to church, Gladys had become friends with Mattie Denson, the wife of the Reverend J. J. Denson, whose younger son, Jesse Lee, was a professional musician. Gladys asked Mrs. Denson if Lee might give Elvis guitar lessons. Lee wasn't exactly overjoyed at the idea, but his mother insisted, and Elvis began going to the Densons' house on the weekends for more advanced guitar lessons.

Years later, Lee would recall: "He had a little itty-bitty, Gene Autry–type guitar that he really couldn't play. He couldn't press the strings down on it they was set so high, so I let him practice on mine. I just tried to show him basic chords. I would take his fingers and place them, say, 'You're pressing the wrong strings with the wrong fingers.' He couldn't really complete a song for a long time . . . but once I straightened him out he started to learn to do it right."

By the tenth grade, Elvis began to come out of his shell. He joined the ROTC and became a library assistant at school. As his lessons with Lee progressed, he began to bring his guitar out and sing for neighbors at the Courts—softly, quietly, his voice just above a whisper, ballads like "Harbor Lights" or "Moonlight Bay."

Elvis soon learned that the guitar attracted girls. And Elvis always liked the girls. He gained a reputation for being a great kisser, and he was always ready to put down the guitar and play spin-the-bottle when the girls came out to listen to him sing.

By his junior year, Elvis began to take more interest in his appearance. In an age where most boys wore their hair short, in flattops or crew cuts, Elvis let his hair grow long and combed it back on the sides to overlap in ducktails, using Rose Oil hair tonic to slick it down. Then he started to grow sideburns so he could look older.

It was also in his junior year that Elvis decided to try out for the Humes football team. It was a short-lived attempt. Some of the other boys on the team ganged up on him in the locker room, held him down, and were going to cut his hair. And they probably would have if Red West, the star of the Humes team, who became a lifelong friend, had not come to his rescue because he "felt sorry for him." But the coach kicked Elvis off the team a couple of days later anyway because he still refused to cut his hair.

It was during Elvis's senior year at Humes that the Presleys were evicted from the Courts, but this time it was not because they couldn't pay the rent but because they were earning too much money. Both Vernon and Gladys had steady jobs. They had bought a car and cleared most of their debts when the Memphis Housing Authority informed them that they were now making more than was allowed for public housing.

It was also around this time Elvis started wearing pink and black shirts with the collar turned up, pleated slacks, and loafers. On his occasional trips down to Beale Street, the home of black music in Memphis, Elvis liked to stop and look in the windows at Lansky's, a clothing store that sold flashy apparel to the black singers.

To help finance his new look, Elvis took a couple of part-time jobs, including one as an usher at Loew's movie house. When he saved enough money, he bought a black bolero jacket, the kind Spanish dancers wear, at Lansky's. When Elvis wore it to school, the other students teased him more, saying he looked like a car-hop at a drive-in. Elvis also developed a swagger to his walk, swiveling his hips ever so slightly. One classmate said he walked like a gunfighter who was about to spin around and draw a six-shooter.

In short, Elvis looked weird. Long hair. Sideburns. Flashy clothes. Wiggle in his walk. But for Elvis at the time, it was all part of a statement he was making. If other students thought he was a freak, he was becoming more confident in his own persona.

Just as Elvis was beginning to shed his shyness through his wardrobe and appearance, he also began to drop his reticence about his music. As graduation approached, Elvis again began to take his guitar to school, and he appeared in the Humes High School Minstrel Show, singing "Till I Waltz Again with You." It was the first time many of his classmates knew he could sing. He even carried his guitar to the school picnic, and while most of the students were off playing games, Elvis sat on a bench and plucked the guitar and sang. Soon he had a small crowd around him, mostly girls, listening.

Elvis graduated from Humes on June 3, 1953. Elvis's parents were so proud they had his diploma framed and hung it on the wall. A month later, he got a job at M. B. Parker Machinists Shop. It paid thirty-six dollars a week.

That summer an article appeared in *The Memphis Press-Scimitar* about a new singing group, The Prisonaires, whose five members were serving time in the Tennessee state prison. What interested Elvis most was the mention of the studio where the record had been made—the Memphis Recording Service—and its proprietor, a man named Sam Phillips, who, it said, had "established a reputation as an expert" in finding new talent.

* * *

Sam Phillips came to the bright lights of Memphis as a young man with a mission. He was passionate about music, specifically the gospel and blues music of African Americans that he had heard in churches and fields while growing up in rural Alabama. Phillips believed that Negro music—as it was called in those days—was the only original American music, and he wanted to make it known to the rest of the country. Phillips also was convinced there was a music that hadn't yet been invented—a sort of hybrid blend of gospel, blues, and country. He wasn't sure what it was, but he knew it was there and that he would know it when he heard it.

As part of fulfilling his dream, Phillips had started the Memphis Recording Service three years earlier, and in an effort to expand he had launched his own record label—Sun Records—as a side business just a few months previously. The only other employee was Marion Keisker, who was a radio personality in her own right and took the job as receptionist and secretary purely and simply because she was in love with Sam Phillips.

Phillips, a native Alabaman, was a slim man with dashing good looks yet with a hint of raw country still about him. He took pains with his appearance, especially his hair, and was always well groomed and well dressed.

Even if Elvis had not seen the story in the paper, he might have heard mention of Sam Phillips and his studio on the nightly radio show hosted by "Daddy-O" Dewey Phillips. The two men shared more than the last name. They both loved the same kind of music, and Dewey Phillips would often give a plug to Sam Phillips's studio on his show.

Whatever the reason, toward the end of that summer, Elvis decided he had to do something about his dreams of being a singer. Nothing ventured, nothing gained.

It was a Saturday in August when an eighteen-year-old Elvis Presley, carrying what looked like a child's guitar, walked into Sam Phillips's studio on Union Street. Marion Keisker looked up and asked if she could help him. Elvis said he wanted to make a record to give to his mother. Marion told him that it was $3.98 for a record, but for one dollar more he could also have a tape. He said he just wanted a record, and began to count out the money.

Marion asked him his name, and then misspelled it on the card she made out when he mumbled his reply. Marion liked the young man, who was so polite and shy yet also intense. While they were waiting to make the record, Elvis asked her if the studio ever needed backup singers for their records. Sometimes, she said.

"What kind of singer are you?" she asked.

"I sing all kinds," Elvis said.

"Who do you sound like?"

"I don't sound like nobody."

"What do you sing? Hillbilly?"

"I sing hillbilly."

"Well, who do you sound like in hillbilly?"

"I don't sound like nobody."

Finally, the studio was ready, and Elvis went in with his guitar and began to sing the main song he had come to record—"My Happiness." It was a ballad he had sung many times on the steps at the Courts, for his mom and her friends, and for the girls. For the flip side he sang "That's When Your Heartaches Begin." Years later, Elvis recalled that his guitar playing "sounded like somebody beatin' on a bucket lid."

Marion had listened in while Elvis made his record, and from the first plaintive, quavering notes that he sang, she realized he was right. He didn't sound like anybody else. At the end of the session, Sam told Elvis he had an "interesting" voice. Elvis hoped he would say more, but Phillips added nothing. After Elvis left, Phillips told Marion to make a note by the boy's name. "Good ballad singer," Marion wrote. "Hold."

Throughout the fall, every time he could pluck up the courage, Elvis would drop by the studio and ask if there was any need for a singer. Marion never had a singing job for him, but she didn't discourage him from coming by either. She had grown quite fond of the boy, and his clear longing to be a singer touched her.

CHAPTER THREE

AROUND THE TIME of his nineteenth birthday in 1954, Elvis fell in love. In addition to the regular services at church, Elvis also attended a Bible study group for young men, known as Christ's Ambassadors. It was while a bunch of kids were standing outside, waiting to split up into boys' and girls' classes, that Dixie Locke first noticed the shy boy with the droopy eyes and pouting lips that were always just about to break into a smile. Although some of the other kids made fun of the way he dressed, she thought he was the sexiest thing she had ever seen.

Dixie was fifteen years old and a sophomore at South Side High. She lived with two older sisters and her parents in a one-bedroom apartment not far from the Presleys. Dixie was attractive and bright, and curious about the boy who wore pink and black shirts, had long hair that he kept combing, and seemed to be constantly drumming his fingers on any surface available.

Although Dixie and Elvis had taken note of each other, and each liked what they saw, it was not proper for a girl to start up a conversation with a strange boy, especially at church. And Elvis was so shy he couldn't go up to a girl to whom he had not been introduced. One Sunday morning, Dixie decided she had to make her move.

As the boys and girls were waiting together before separating, Dixie began to tell the girls around her that she was going roller-skating that weekend. She spoke loudly and deliberately so that the boys standing nearby would be sure to hear her. Then she waited.

Sure enough! That Saturday night, Elvis showed up at the roller rink. He was wearing his black bolero jacket with a ruffled shirt and black pants with a pink stripe down the leg. He had skates on, but he was holding on to the railing for dear life.

Dixie suddenly realized that he didn't know how to skate. Finally she skated up to him and introduced herself. Elvis smiled sheepishly and said, yeah, he knew who she was, and asked her if she would like a soda.

The two of them went to the snack area and began to talk. They talked and talked and talked. They never did go back to the skating rink, and when the session ended, Elvis asked if she would like to go to a drive-in.

Elvis drove to K's, a popular hangout for teenagers, and as they sat in the car eating their burgers and slurping their shakes, Elvis told her how he wanted to be a singer. He had never admitted this to any of his friends or family before. He told her about his love of music, and just about everything else in his life. They talked for hours, and before they drove home, Dixie kissed him. At the front door, Elvis had told her he would call her next week, and maybe they could go out the following weekend.

He called her the next day.

When it came time for Elvis to meet her parents, Dixie was nervous. There was no escaping the fact that Elvis looked different. She kept emphasizing to her mother and father that she had met him at church. In the end, Elvis's politeness—his soft-spoken "no, sir" and "yes, ma'am" to all of the Lockes' questions—won the day.

For the next few months, Elvis and Dixie were in-

Elvis escorted Dixie Locke, his first true love, to her junior prom, but his success would later put strains on their relationship.

separable. They went everywhere together—to church, to the movies, to the All-Night Gospel concerts at Ellis Auditorium, to K's drive-in, and to Charlie's Record Shop, a familiar hangout for Elvis but new territory for Dixie. The store had a jukebox and a soda fountain and listening booths, and the kids from the neighborhood sometimes spent hours there playing the latest records. It was there that Elvis played for Dixie the original of one of the songs he often sang to her, Lonnie Johnson's "Tomorrow Night."

They went out almost every night, and by the spring, they were often ending up at Riverside Park, a lover's lane for teenagers in Memphis. The relationship became passionate very quickly, but both Elvis and Dixie agreed that they would not go all the way until they were married. And they began to talk about marriage, sometimes discussing running away to Mississippi. But in the end, they always decided to wait.

In April, Elvis changed jobs. He had heard about an opening at the Crown Electric Company for a truck driver, and went to apply. The wife of the owner, Gladys Tipler, was impressed by his politeness, and they hired him. His new salary was higher, forty dollars a week. Every payday, Elvis would bring his check home and give it to his father. Elvis would keep back a few dollars for his own expenses—gas for the car, some money to take Dixie to the movies and buy a hamburger afterward—but the rest went to his family.

All his free time, he spent with Dixie. Elvis felt that Dixie, unlike his past girlfriends or even the other boys from the Courts, understood him, and he could open up his heart and talk to her about his innermost feelings. If her family or friends teased her about Elvis—about his hair, his clothes, the way he constantly tapped his fingers—Dixie would defend him vehemently. Elvis wasn't phony, and he wasn't a show-off. Dixie knew that deep down inside, Elvis was just a nice boy who desperately wanted to please people.

Although Elvis had talked to Dixie about his dream of being a singer, it was still a surprise when one day in May Elvis told her he had heard that Eddie Bond, a band leader at a local nightclub, was looking for a singer, and he had decided to try out.

The next week, Dixie went with Elvis to the Hi-Hat Club for his audition for Eddie Bond. For the occasion, Elvis wore his black bolero jacket with a pink shirt.

He had even gotten a haircut. Bond came over to the table where they were sitting and introduced himself. He asked Elvis if he had a job, and Elvis told him he drove a truck for Crown Electric. A few minutes later, it was Elvis's turn to go onstage.

He sang two songs, accompanied only by himself on his guitar. When it was over, he and Bond talked briefly by the side of the stage. When Elvis returned he told Dixie to get her things, they were leaving. Elvis never told Dixie what Bond said, and she didn't ask. But it was clear Elvis was dejected. Years later, Elvis confided to a friend that Bond told him he should stick to driving a truck, because he would never make it as a singer.

After the episode at the Hi-Hat Club, Elvis began to train as an electrician because he didn't want to end up being a truck driver for the rest of his life. Despite the failed audition, he still nourished his dream of being a singer. He even carried his guitar with him on his delivery rounds.

Dixie was supposed to go with her parents to Florida on two weeks' vacation at the beginning of July. It would be the first time she and Elvis were separated since they had started going together. At the end of June, a week before Dixie was to leave, Elvis had a telephone call out of the blue from Marion Keisker at Sun Records.

Sam Phillips, the studio owner, had been given a demo record of a new song that Sam thought had possibilities. It just needed the right singer. Sam asked Marion the name of that kid with the high-pitched voice who kept coming by. "Elvis Presley," Marion said. Marion called Elvis and asked if he could stop by the studio that afternoon. As Elvis recalled later, "I was there by the time she hung up the phone."

Sam had Elvis go over the new song all afternoon, and when it became clear that he wasn't going to get it right, he had Elvis sing just about every other song he knew. Elvis sang for Sam for hours, and at the end, he was exhausted. Sam recalled thinking that while Elvis wasn't much of a guitar player, there was something in his voice—a need to communicate—that came from deep inside.

At the end of the session, nothing was said about what might happen next. Sam thanked Elvis. He thought that they just hadn't found the right song for his voice. But the voice haunted him. Elvis was happy that someone had listened to him.

Dixie left with her parents for Florida on July 2. Elvis came over to see them off, and he and Dixie had a tearful parting, promising to write every day. But those two weeks would change both their lives forever.

On the weekend Dixie left, Elvis had another telephone call. This one was from a guitarist named Scotty Moore, a twenty-two-year-old guitar player who had a group called the Starlite Wranglers, a hillbilly band that played clubs on the weekends. But Scotty had larger ambitions. Sam liked Scotty and knew the guitarist was looking for something bigger than the Wranglers. Sam mentioned a young singer with a quavering voice who had been in the studio earlier in the week, and suggested Scotty listen to him and see what he thought. Scotty asked Elvis to come over the next day and also invited Bill Black, who played bass, to join them.

Elvis arrived dressed in a black shirt and pink pants. The three of them chatted for a bit—Scotty and Bill did most of the talking—and then they had him sing a few songs. He seemed to know every song ever recorded. In the end, however, neither Scotty nor Bill thought he was that special, although they had to admit the kid had a nice voice. Despite their lack of enthusiasm, Sam wanted to set up a session for the three of them the next night.

The session began at seven P.M. Elvis was clearly nervous when he arrived. Sam, Scotty, and Bill engaged in some small talk to try to put him at ease, but Elvis was mostly silent. Then Sam turned to him and said, "What do you want to sing?" They settled on "Harbor Lights" and went through that a few times. Then they did "I Love You Because," another ballad that had been a big hit a few years earlier.

They played the songs at different tempos, over and over, each time trying to make them sound new and fresh. Elvis was beginning to get frustrated. After what seemed like hours, Sam came out and told them to take a break. Elvis and Scotty and Bill got sodas, and Sam went back into the control room but left the door open.

While they were drinking their sodas, a song came into Elvis's head that he used to sing at the Courts. The song was "That's All Right, Mama," an old blues number by Arthur "Big Boy" Crudup. Elvis started to sing and jump around the studio. Bill and Scotty began to play along. They were just cutting up, unwinding before the session resumed.

Sam suddenly appeared in the door to the control room and asked, "What are you doing?" They all stopped and said, "We don't know." But Sam was excited. "Well, back up, find a place to start, and do it again," he said.

They did it again. And again. And again. They worked on it for the rest of the night. It opened with Elvis's rhythm guitar chords, followed by his voice, growing in confidence with each take, coming in on the vocals, then Scotty and Bill picking up on the background. When they played back the tape of the final cut, they all were excited.

Sam told the three young men to come back the next night for another session. For two consecutive nights, they tried several other songs, but nothing worked. Finally, Sam called an end to the sessions.

After Elvis and Scotty and Bill left on the Wednesday, Sam sat alone in his studio. He still had no doubts about what had happened on the first night. That was the music he had dreamed about. Only time would tell whether that first session had been just a stroke of luck or whether they would be able to repeat it. But he believed enough in what they had to call his friend Dewey Phillips at the radio station and ask him to come by after his show that night.

Daddy-O Dewey would often drop by Sam's studio for a late-night beer and talk that would sometimes go on until dawn. On this night, however, Sam had something he especially wanted Dewey to hear. He played the tape of "That's All Right, Mama" several times. Dewey listened. He knew the song well. But something about this version intrigued him. In the end, Dewey didn't have much to say, and the two men parted early.

The next morning Sam had a phone call from Dewey. Daddy-O said he hadn't been able to sleep all night. That song Sam had played for him kept going over and over in his head. He said he wanted to play it on his show.

Sam called Elvis to tell him Daddy-O Dewey was going to play "That's All Right, Mama" that night! As the hour for the broadcast approached, Elvis tuned the family radio to Dewey's station and told Vernon and Gladys to keep listening. Then Elvis went to the movies.

It was about a half hour into the show that Dewey announced he was going to spin a new record, and proceeded to play "That's All Right, Mama" several times in a row. Some say seven times in a row; some say eleven times. However many times, the response was immediate. The station switchboard lit up with scores of calls from listeners wanting to know where they could buy it.

The Presleys, listening at home, were stunned. Gladys said later that the biggest shock for her was "hearing them say his name over the radio." They didn't have long to absorb the shock. The telephone at home began to ring as well. The first call was from Dewey asking for Elvis. Gladys, who answered the phone, told Dewey that Elvis was at the movies. Dewey told her to find him and get him down to his studio. "I played that record of his and the birdbrain phones haven't stopped ringing since," Dewey said.

Gladys and Vernon raced to the theater and found Elvis sitting in the dark. They took him to the studio, and Dewey said he was going to interview him. Years later, Elvis recalled: "I was scared to death. I was shaking all over. I just couldn't believe it."

Elvis told Dewey he didn't know anything about being interviewed, and Dewey told him to relax and they would rehearse it a bit, he just shouldn't say anything dirty. So Dewey began asking Elvis questions. After a few minutes, Dewey thanked him and told him he could leave. Elvis asked, "Aren't you going to interview me?" "I just have," Dewey replied. "The mike's been open the whole time."

As Elvis himself would later tell it, about a year after cutting his first demo record for his mom, he was an overnight sensation.

CHAPTER FOUR

THE INSTANT SUCCESS "That's All Right, Mama" had on the radio created an immediate problem for Sam Phillips. Before he could put a record into stores, he had to have a Side B. The next day he called Elvis, Scotty, and Bill back into the studio to try to find a suitable song for the flip side. One problem was that while Elvis knew maybe the first verse and the chorus of nearly every song recorded in the past decade, he didn't know any of them all the way through.

The three young men spent the whole weekend in the studio, going from one song to the next, but never finding anything that really worked. By the end of their third night, they were beginning to wonder whether "That's All Right, Mama" had just been some kind of accident. Once again, Sam called a break. Once again, it was while they were clowning around that inspiration struck. This time it was Bill Black who started the ball rolling.

Bill started slapping his bass and singing in a high falsetto voice a song that had been a big hit a few years earlier called "Blue Moon of Kentucky." Elvis picked it up and took over the singing. Suddenly Sam was back at the control room door telling them to try that again.

The result turned "Blue Moon of Kentucky" from a slow waltz-like ballad into an upbeat rock song. Sam also decided to mix in a sort of echoing device that not only enhanced the recording but covered up some mistakes in the playing.

Sam knew he had a hit. When the record was officially released a week later as Sun Records No. 209, he already had orders for six thousand copies. Promoters called wanting to book the trio for public appearances, and there had been calls from local entrepreneurs wanting to know if Elvis had a manager and offering their services if he didn't. Sam asked Scotty if he would act as Elvis's manager. Elvis had never even thought of having a manager and readily agreed to let Scotty be his.

is, Bill Black, and Scotty Moore posed with Sam Phillips at Sun Records after their t single came out in 1954.

Scotty and Bill's other group, the Starlite Wranglers, had a regular weekend gig at a bar called the Bon Air, and Sam decided that Elvis's first appearance would be there the following Saturday night as a special act at intermission. For the first time, Sam took a hard look at Elvis and began to wonder what kind of impression he would make onstage with his pink and black outfits and long hair, especially at a club filled with beer-drinking rednecks in jeans and cowboy hats who were there to hear twangy hillbilly music.

For nineteen-year-old Elvis, the summer of 1954 was racing forward like an express train. Every day, he wished he could call Dixie and tell her the news. But Dixie was still on vacation in Florida with her family, and he didn't have a phone number for her. In the end he sent a telegram to an address he had for her cousin. It said simply: "HURRY HOME. MY RECORD IS DOING GREAT." Dixie had no idea what he was talking about.

On Saturday night, Sam drove Elvis to the Bon Air Club. They sat at a table in the corner while the Wranglers performed their first set. Sam could sense that Elvis was getting more and more nervous. Then he got up with Scotty and Bill and sang his two songs—they were the only two in his repertory—and it was all over.

The crowd had listened to him and given him polite applause. But they hadn't booed or thrown anything at him. And for Sam, that was enough. He was already working on another engagement that would be more of a test of Elvis's stage presence. Elvis, on the other hand, thought his appearance at the Bon Air had been a failure, and as they drove home, Sam felt Elvis's confidence deflate, like air seeping out of a balloon.

For the next two weeks, life went on as it had before. Elvis worked during the day and rehearsed with Scotty and Bill at night. When Dixie returned home, everything seemed unchanged. But she already realized that it was not quite the same.

The other big engagement that Sam had been working on was for Elvis to appear at an outdoor concert being organized by Bob Neal, another disc jockey in Memphis, for a big amphitheater in Overton Park at the end of the month. The main attraction was to be Slim Whitman, a star of the Louisiana Hayride, a radio program that was second only to the Grand Ole Opry in popularity. Neal, who was well aware of the splash Elvis's record was making around town, agreed to put Elvis on the program.

The concert was on a Friday night at the end of July. Dixie drove Elvis to the park, and she could tell how nervous he was because he couldn't stop fidgeting.

When they arrived, the park was already packed. Elvis became even more jumpy when he couldn't find Sam Phillips. Sam, who had been held up in traffic, was somewhat alarmed when he arrived late and saw how tense Elvis was. Elvis was even stuttering.

When Elvis went onstage, his knees were literally knocking together. He grabbed the microphone to adjust it as though he were choking it. Then he stepped back and struck the opening chord of "That's All Right, Mama." He stepped up on the balls of his feet, leaning into the microphone, and his lips curled into a sort of pout as he sang. Then he began to shake his leg, ever so slightly, to keep time with the music. Suddenly the audience was shouting. As Elvis recalled later, "Everybody was hollering and I didn't know what they were hollering at."

At first, Elvis thought they were making fun of him. But when he launched into "Blue Moon of Kentucky," he jiggled his leg some more and the audience screamed even louder. The crowd called him back for an encore, but since those were the only two songs the trio had rehearsed, Elvis just sang a reprise of "Blue Moon of Kentucky." By this time he had figured out what the audience—the girls especially—were screaming at, and he wiggled his legs even more. With each shake of the leg, Elvis's confidence grew. In an interview later, Elvis explained, "The more I did, the wilder they went."

The reaction to the Overton Park show was beyond Sam Phillips's wildest expectations. Even Bob Neal and Slim Whitman, who had been standing in the wings waiting to go on, were surprised. The cheers that followed Elvis from the stage were no illusion. Sam knew that Elvis was bound for stardom.

The one person in the audience that day who had mixed emotions about Elvis's showstopping performance was Dixie. Years later, looking back on that hot July day, she said she wanted to tell all the other girls who were screaming to shut up and leave him alone. She also realized that he was doing what he had always dreamed of doing, and he loved it. And it didn't involve her.

For the next several weeks, Sam Phillips hit the road. In the days before the Web, when anyone can download a song onto an iPod, about the only way to hear new songs was over the radio. And since most radio stations had a broadcast range of only a few miles, a big hit in Memphis could remain unknown to the rest of the country unless DJs at other radio stations got a copy and started playing it for their audiences. Sun Records didn't have sales reps, so Sam loaded his car with demos of Sun No. 209 and started traveling through the South, from Georgia to Mississippi, Louisiana, and on to Texas, meeting with disc jockeys, jukebox operators, and record-store owners, playing Elvis's song for them and trying to spread the word about the new music.

The fact that it was such new music, a crossover between white country western and black rhythm and blues, was one of the biggest problems he faced. When he went into black radio stations, the disc jockeys thought the music sounded too country. When he went into white radio stations, they thought it was too R&B.

But Sam was a patient man. He kept explaining to one DJ after another that this was the new beat and there was no stopping it. It was the big cities that first gave it air time. When stations in Dallas, Houston, and Atlanta played the record—both sides of it—they were flooded with calls from their teenage listeners.

At the end of the summer the big breakthrough came. In the August 28, 1954, edition of *Billboard* magazine a new name entered the list of top-ten recording artists. Elvis Presley was the number 3 singer in the regional best sellers. Since there was no category to cover his music, it was listed in the country western category. And the song was not "That's All Right, Mama," but the flip side—"Blue Moon of Kentucky."

It was just one line in *Billboard*'s regional lists, but Elvis Presley was now on the charts. It was enough for Sam Phillips to call Jim Denny, the manager of the Grand Ole Opry, and ask him to give Elvis a spot. Denny said he would think about it.

While all this was going on, Elvis still drove his truck for Crown Electric during the day, but most of his nights were taken up rehearsing with Scotty and Bill, trying to find new songs. There was also a follow-up record to think about, and they knew Sam would want to go back into the studio to cut one once he returned from his road trip.

The trio started playing a regular weekend date at the Eagle's Nest Club. It was still only an intermission appearance in which Elvis would sing the two songs they knew. But more and more people were coming to the club just for that intermission show. The trio also had an appearance at the opening of a shopping center, and when word got around that Elvis was going to sing, hundreds of people—mostly teenagers—showed up.

For the most part, the summer glided by. But there was a tension in the air, even on the nights when they would just sit around trying out new songs. There was a sense that this was just a lull in the action and the fireworks were going to start soon.

For Dixie, it was a happy time but also one of foreboding. She and Elvis still went out. But Dixie knew that the craze wasn't going to end, that at some point she was going to lose him to his fans. She began to realize that she might never be Mrs. Elvis Presley.

Toward the end of September, Sam Phillips had a call from Nashville. Jim Denny told Sam that he could give Elvis a one-shot appearance on next Saturday's Grand Ole Opry, if they could get to Nashville. Denny said the trio could perform one song—their up-tempo version of "Blue Moon of Kentucky." Sam said they would be there.

CHAPTER FIVE

DURING THE LAST weeks of that summer, Elvis and Scotty and Bill were in Sam's studio every spare moment trying to get two more songs together for another record. It was a frustrating time since Sam had a definite idea of what he wanted for the follow-up single, but he wasn't hearing it in any of the songs the trio was playing.

Occasionally, they would start out on a number only to be interrupted by Sam who would come out of the control room and tell them that wasn't quite right, but then turn to Elvis and say, "Just keep what you did there." Elvis, who wasn't sure about anything anymore, would frantically ask, "What did I do? What did I do?"

In the sessions, Elvis went through a catalogue of songs, most of which eventually ended up on records:

"Blue Moon," again using an echo effect with Elvis singing falsetto; "Tomorrow Night," the old Lonnie Johnson ballad that was one of Elvis's favorite songs; "Just Because," a country number first recorded by the Lone Star Cowboys in 1933.

Finally, a week before their scheduled appearance on the Grand Ole Opry, Sam issued a new Sun single. The last song in their recording session had been a cover of "Good Rockin' Tonight," and Sam made it the lead side. For the flip side Sam chose the trio's rendition of "I Don't Care If the Sun Don't Shine," a song Mack David wrote for the Disney movie *Cinderella*, but which didn't make the film's final score and was later recorded by Dean Martin.

But it was "Good Rockin' Tonight" that carried the message Sam wanted to deliver with Elvis's second single. From Elvis's first words, the song was like a declaration of independence for the new rock and roll, the music Sam knew was the wave of the future and for which Elvis would be the prophet.

On Saturday morning, October 2, 1954, Elvis, Scotty, and Bill piled into Sam's 1951 Cadillac and drove two hundred miles across the state of Tennessee for their one-song appearance on the Grand Ole Opry that night.

It's hard to exaggerate what this engagement meant to the three young men. All of them had grown up in a Southern culture where listening to the Opry on the radio on Saturday night was almost a ritual. If Elvis had been nervous playing honky-tonks and outdoor concerts in Memphis, Sam expected him to be petrified for this performance. Playing the Opry was a different league from playing for the opening of a supermarket.

Oddly, it was Elvis who sort of took charge once they arrived at the auditorium. Scotty and Bill, both of whom regarded that night as the possible pinnacle of their careers, stood immobile as they watched the biggest stars of country music wander around backstage before the show.

Elvis went up to everybody he recognized, and, polite as always, introduced himself. At one point he spotted Chet Atkins, and said, "Mr. Atkins, my guitar player wants to meet you," then pulled Scotty over to meet the great guitarist. Elvis was still nervous, but he was clearly enjoying the experience. It was almost as if a Little League baseball player had found himself at Yankee Stadium for an All-Star game and was going around introducing himself to Mickey Mantle, Willie Mays, and Ted Williams.

The trio had their own cheering section from Memphis in the audience. Scotty and Bill had told their wives, Bobbie and Evelyn, that there was no room for them to come along, but the two women decided about noon that day to drive over themselves to see the show. Likewise, Sam had left Marion Keisker behind to look after the studio. But she locked the doors and took a bus over to Nashville.

When time came for Elvis's number, the big country-music star Hank Snow was supposed to introduce him. But he forgot Elvis's name and introduced him simply as a new singer from Memphis. It didn't bother Elvis. He bounced out on the stage, grabbed the mike, and sang his one song. When he finished, the audience gave him a polite round of applause, and it was over.

Sam conferred afterward with Jim Denny, who told him that while Elvis's music wasn't exactly in the Opry tradition, "this boy is not bad." If Elvis, Scotty, and Bill were a bit downcast, Sam was elated. Denny, whatever his taste in music, knew talent, and he had volunteered praise of Elvis. And despite the reception they had from the audience, just playing the Grand Ole Opry was good for any musician's résumé.

On the Monday after their return, Sam called Pappy Covington of the Louisiana Hayride—a more free-spirited cousin of the Opry that had a reputation for encouraging new talent—and got Elvis and the trio a booking for two weeks later. The Louisiana Hayride, the second most popular country-music show, broadcast out of Shreveport, and had two shows every Saturday night. The first one was broadcast live over the radio. A later show was for a theater audience only.

Sam, Elvis, Scotty, and Bill drove down to northwest Louisiana in Sam's car. Elvis was once again visibly nervous. When the trio came onstage, his legs were shaking. As he sang, he leaned so far forward, it seemed like he might fall over into the audience.

The audience's reaction for the live radio performance was much the same as it had been in Nashville at the Opry—polite but less than overwhelming. Sam went backstage between shows to talk to Elvis. He found him standing alone and dejected in a corner.

Sam told Elvis to forget about the audience and just do his own thing. When Sam went back to take his seat, he noticed that a lot of younger people from the first show had stayed for the second, and there were also more teenagers in this audience.

Whatever Sam said, it worked. Elvis was more himself when the trio came out for the second show, and the reaction was totally different. After they got through the first number, the entire audience was on its feet cheering. One woman turned to Sam, not knowing who he was, and said, "Man, have you ever heard anything like that?" Then she started jumping up and down and screaming.

At the end of the second show, Pappy Covington told Sam that he would like Elvis and the trio to become regulars on the Hayride. When they got back to Memphis, all three decided to quit their day jobs and devote themselves full-time to their music. When Elvis told his dad he was going to quit Crown Electric, Vernon looked at him and said: "You should make up your mind either about being an electrician or playing a guitar. I never saw a guitar player that was worth a damn."

As a gift to himself, Elvis took the money he had made with his Opry and Hayride appearances and bought himself a new guitar—a Martin D-18. He felt guilty about spending so much money on a new guitar, but he told himself that was how he was now going to make his living, and the expense was worth it. He paid $175 for the guitar and gave up his old guitar on a trade-in. The man at the guitar shop gave him eight dollars for his old guitar, then promptly threw it in the trash. It hurt Elvis's feelings to see his old guitar go into a garbage can, and when he told the story in later years, he would shake his head and say, "Shucks, it still played good." Elvis had his name spelled out on his new guitar in black metallic letters, just below the fret board. It was a name that was becoming more and more familiar.

At the end of October, Elvis and Scotty and Bill signed a contract as regulars on the Louisiana Hayride. Elvis got eighteen dollars a show as singer and Scotty and Bill received twelve dollars each. But with the exposure from the Hayride, they began to get other bookings as well.

One benefit of the one-night stands was that in each

town they were scheduled to appear, the local radio station would play their records for days in advance, which meant more record sales. Also, there would often be stories in local newspapers about him, and Elvis would clip them out and send them home. Gladys and Dixie, who now spent a lot of time together, would paste them in a scrapbook.

The length of the commute to Shreveport for the Louisiana Hayride, however, meant that Elvis and Scotty and Bill often stayed overnight there rather than drive home after each performance. And with the extra gigs in other towns, Elvis was spending more and more time on the road and less and less time in Memphis. Dixie could feel Elvis slipping away from her. When they would go out now in Memphis, there were groups of fans—girls mostly—who gathered around him, and she could tell Elvis enjoyed it.

And it wasn't only girls who were starting to pay more attention. Bob Neal, the Memphis disc jockey who had booked Elvis into the Overton Park concert, called Sam Phillips and asked if Elvis had a manager. Sam told him that Scotty had been handling the trio's bookings, but they had no real manager. Neal said he could get them even more engagements at better venues, and everyone agreed to have Neal be their manager.

Dixie had been looking forward to her and Elvis's first Christmas together. But Elvis didn't arrive home from the weekly Hayride show until Christmas Eve, and then he told Dixie he had to leave the day after Christmas for an appearance at the Houston Hoedown. Then he had another show at a special New Year's jamboree. The roller coaster was starting to zoom downhill.

Throughout that winter, Elvis, Scotty, and Bill were on the road. They would often play two or three shows a day in some small town, then drive all night to appear at a concert in a big city. And Sam Phillips was pushing out the records. In December he issued Elvis's third single with "Milkcow Blues Boogie" and "You're a Heartbreaker."

And Elvis worked on his act. He kept trying different moves onstage to get the reaction from the audience. He was a quick learner. If girls screamed at some particular move, Elvis would repeat it in the next show. If some move didn't get a response, he would drop it. He found especially that when he swiveled his hips, the girls in the audience would go wild. It was the quality that Dixie had first seen in him. Elvis just wanted to please people, and if shaking his leg and his hips while he sang made the girls squeal with delight, he would keep on doing it.

During those weeks on the road, Elvis called his mother and Dixie every night after the show. Often Dixie would be at the Presleys' house, waiting for his call. Dixie and Gladys became very close during those months. They were happy for Elvis, but each worried that his growing fame would change him.

With all the extra shows they were playing, the trio also was beginning to make some money at last. For the first time in his life, Elvis didn't have to count every nickel. He saved some of what he got for each show and sent it home to his parents. In January 1955, as a sort of twentieth birthday present to himself, Elvis bought a car. It was a used 1951 Lincoln, and he had the sides painted with the legend "Elvis Presley—Sun Records."

Bob Neal was as good as his word about getting Elvis into bigger shows. Neal quickly booked the trio into appearances across the Southwest, ending up with a couple of concerts in Memphis. Neal also contacted Colonel Thomas A. Parker, a big-time promoter, to see if he would add Elvis, Scotty, and Bill to a tour Parker was putting together.

At Memphis, Neal arranged a meeting between Parker and Sam Phillips at a restaurant. Neal knew that even his connections were limited, and if Elvis was going to reach a national audience he would need someone with contacts in New York and California. Parker had those.

Parker's background was always a little vague. The story about him was that he had grown up in an orphanage, but he had run away and joined a circus. Later he had a business running a pet cemetery in Florida and worked as a dogcatcher and as a local press agent for several big-name country singers when they toured the state. In fact, he had been born in Holland and came to America working on a merchant ship.

His big claim to fame was as Eddy Arnold's manager. He had turned Arnold from a singer on the Grand Ole Opry into a TV and movie star and a headliner in Las Vegas nightclubs. Then, for reasons that are obscure, Arnold fired him. Parker was now Hank Snow's manager and ran an enterprise called Jamboree Attractions that organized tours featuring the top country singers. It was through his music connections that he persuaded Jimmie Davis, a former country singing star who became governor of Louisiana and was famous for the song "You Are My Sunshine," to make him an honorary colonel in the state. From then on, he insisted everyone call him "the Colonel."

Parker, a bearish man with bushy eyebrows who looked a little like a leprechaun, had agreed to add Elvis to a tour that was starting in a week, but if Neal was hoping Parker and Phillips would find common cause in helping to promote Elvis into the big time, he was quickly disillusioned. Phillips and Parker took an instant dislike to each other. It began even as Neal made the introductions. Parker, chewing on a cigar, told Phillips to call him "the Colonel." Phillips kept calling him "Mr. Parker."

Parker then proceeded to tell both Neal and Phillips that Elvis would never go anywhere as long as he stayed with Sun Records. What Elvis needed was to be with a big label like RCA, which had national distri-

After Colonel Tom Parker began to handle Elvis's business interests in 1955, the entrepreneur quickly moved to change all his contracts.

bution and could get the records into stores from New York to California. Phillips knew it was true, but he was seething with anger.

But what really defined the antipathy between the two men was even more fundamental. Parker made no secret of the fact that he didn't particularly like the new music that Elvis was singing, but he could see that the boy had potential as an entertainer. For Phillips, this was the music he had dreamed about making, and Elvis would carry it to the world. In short, Phillips was in it for the music, while Parker was in it for the money.

During the week before the tour, Phillips had the trio in the studio every day, trying to find the right songs for a new single. They found one song immediately, a revised version of "Baby, Let's Play House." Elvis opened the song with a sort of hiccupping stutter repeating the word "baby" five times and everyone was knocked out. But by the time the trio left for the tour, they still hadn't found a Side B.

While they were on tour, Bob Neal had arranged for them to appear at a concert in Cleveland, and they drove there the day after they got home. This would be the first time Elvis had appeared outside the South, and Neal wanted to see the reaction to him in a Northern city like Cleveland, which was an important venue for the new music that Elvis represented. Alan Freed, a white disc jockey and concert organizer, had found a growing white audience in Cleveland for black singers like Fats Domino, Joe Turner, and other rhythm and blues performers. Freed, who had since moved on to New York City, was credited with having coined the phrase "rock and roll," which was just coming into use.

Elvis was not totally unknown in Cleveland. Radio stations played his records. But Sun had no distribution in the North and no sales to speak of, so few people in Cleveland knew Elvis's name.

If Bob Neal had any doubts about the reception Elvis would receive in Cleveland, they were quickly put to rest. The audience went wild. All the records they had packed into the trunk of the car were sold, and the local radio stations lined up to interview Elvis.

The Cleveland concert encouraged Neal to shoot for the big time, and he managed to get Elvis, Scotty, and Bill an audition in New York for *Arthur Godfrey's Talent Scouts*, a weekly television talent show that was a sort of forerunner to *American Idol*. Neal was excited. This could be Elvis's big break.

The audition was in March 1955. It was the first time Elvis had ever flown in an airplane, and it was the first time any of the trio had been to New York. They spent a day sightseeing, looking up at the skyscrapers, and riding the subway. When they went into the studio for their audition, however, the balloon burst. The reception they got was cool, if not ice cold. They never even met Arthur Godfrey, and the woman who held the tryout gave them the usual, "Don't call us, we'll call you." It stung Elvis, and in years to come he would often refer to the fact that he was turned down by Arthur Godfrey.

But the trio had little time to think about it. Neal had them booked solidly for the next month, and they had a new car to get them from town to town. Elvis's Lincoln had been totaled in a wreck two months after he bought it. Bill had been driving to a show late one night and had run the car under a hay truck. Elvis didn't blame Bill, but he was disappointed over the loss of the car. He compensated by buying a car that would become a sort of trademark—a 1954 pink Cadillac. Once again he had "Elvis Presley—Sun Records" painted on the side, and he was so proud of it he refused to let anyone smoke inside it.

While they had been on the road, Sam Phillips had found what he hoped would be the song for their next single. Once they were back in Memphis, they recorded a new song called "I'm Left, You're Right, She's Gone." Phillips brought in a drummer for the first time, and Elvis once again used his hiccup break in the lyrics.

The song had been written by Stan Kesler and Bill

Taylor and was based on a Campbell's Soup commercial. Unlike many of the upcoming rock-and-roll singers of the day and the generation that would follow, Elvis didn't write his own songs. But the originality he brought to those he covered—songs that had been recorded by others—was so imaginative and creative that he made them seem new. Later, when songs were written just for him, Colonel Parker insisted that the writers share credits with Elvis because his performance of the songs was so innovative.

It was toward the end of Colonel Parker's second tour, in May 1955, that Elvis played the Gator Bowl concert in Jacksonville at which the girls tore his clothes off him and that vaulted him into national headlines.

Until then, Colonel Parker had been somewhat ambivalent about Elvis. He recognized Elvis's growing popularity, especially among the girls, and the raw energy the young singer brought to the stage. But he wasn't sure that Elvis wasn't just a flash in the pan, a passing fad whose attraction would fade as quickly as it had exploded.

When Mae Axton, the tour's advance woman,

and the Colonel stood in the Gator Bowl locker room watching the girls try to tear Elvis's pants off him, Mae glanced at Parker. As she later recalled, the Colonel had "dollar marks in his eyes."

At the end of the tour, Elvis came home for a two-week vacation. With the news of the Jacksonville riot in all the papers, Elvis was suddenly a celebrity. The crowds that followed him around were bigger, and he was recognized by strangers on the street.

But just coming home was another change for Elvis. Thanks to the money he had been sending his parents, they had moved into a new house. At the time Elvis arrived for his vacation, they still did not have a telephone installed. The next-door neighbors, the Bakers, invited them to use their phone, and for the two weeks he was back in Memphis, Elvis spent almost as much time at the Bakers' talking on the phone as he did at home.

Most of the calls for Elvis were from Colonel Parker, who by now was very interested in him. Although Bob Neal was still Elvis's manager, Parker told Elvis that he was destined for greater things. Elvis was eager to listen, and he kept telling his parents all the things the Colonel could do for him. Parker had connections in TV, in Hollywood, in Las Vegas, he said, and could open doors for him that no one else could.

But Gladys and Vernon were suspicious of the Colonel. It was not just that there was something of a snake-oil salesman about him, but they also didn't like the lifestyle that Elvis was beginning to lead, especially after the Jacksonville riot, and they thought Parker was partly responsible.

Since Elvis was still under twenty-one, Gladys and Vernon would have to sign any formal agreement with Parker, so Elvis kept pleading with his parents, like a child begging for candy, telling them what a powerful and smart man the Colonel was.

Throughout that summer, Elvis's mind seemed to be somewhere in the future. He took Dixie to her junior prom and saw her every day. But when they went out, he seemed to prefer being with other people to being alone with her. He bought himself another new guitar—a Martin-28—and another new Cadillac, this one pink and black.

Sam Phillips had the trio back into the studio for another recording session. Elvis didn't like the first song Sam had them play, which was another original number. It was too slow. But Sam again brought in a drummer, and he had him pick up the tempo so that "I Forgot to Remember to Forget" suddenly sounded twice as fast as it was written and Elvis loved it then. There was no problem with the second song. It was one that Little Junior Parker had cut for Sam two years earlier, a pure rhythm-based blues number and a natural for Elvis. "Mystery Train" was probably the best thing Elvis ever recorded for Sam Phillips.

Back on the road, it was quickly clear that Jacksonville had not been a one-time fluke. Girls screamed and again tried to tear Elvis's clothes off him. The near-riots at the concerts made Gladys and Vernon even more uneasy about where stardom was leading their son. But Elvis begged for them to sign a deal with Colonel Parker. Parker himself began a campaign with the Presleys. He told Vernon how much money he was going to make for Elvis, and he told Gladys that he could protect Elvis from the girls.

Between Elvis's pleading and the Colonel's cajoling, the Presleys finally gave in. In August, Gladys and Vernon signed an agreement naming Parker a "special adviser" to Elvis Presley with exclusive rights to one hundred appearances a year and territorial rights to some fifty cities, including New York, Chicago, Las Vegas, and Los Angeles, and most places in between, with a clause giving Parker the right "to negotiate all renewals on existing contracts." That meant that when Bob Neal's or Sam Phillips's contracts were up, it would be Parker who would decide whether to renew them.

For all practical purposes, Colonel Parker now owned Elvis.

CHAPTER SIX

THE COLONEL WASTED no time taking charge. One of the first things he did—although it was Bob Neal who had to break the news to them—was to change the financial arrangements for the trio. Scotty and Bill were to be put on a straight salary rather than sharing in the fees for each appearance.

Under the old agreement, Elvis got 50 percent of the payment while Scotty and Bill got 25 percent each. Since they had added a drummer, D.J. Fontana, he had been paid a hundred dollars a week salary. Now Scotty and Bill would be on salary, too. Scotty and Bill were not too happy about it, but the truth was that the fans were not flocking to hear Scotty and Bill and D.J. play guitar, bass, and drums. In fact, the Colonel

Elvis's three appearances on The Ed Sullivan Show *earned some of the highest ratings in television history.*

floated the idea of firing all three musicians and using Hank Snow's band to back Elvis up. But Neal vetoed that suggestion even before it got to Elvis, who would not have been happy with it.

Parker concentrated most of his energy on breaking Elvis's contract with Sam Phillips and Sun Records. Even Sam Phillips knew he would not be able to keep Elvis much longer. Sun could never give Elvis's records the national distribution that the big labels could. Sam had always known that Sun could not survive on just one star, even one like Elvis. During the past year, Sam had already signed up a couple of other promising artists—a door-to-door appliance salesman named Johnny Cash who, like Elvis, had stopped by his studio asking for an audition, and Carl Perkins, whose "Blue Suede Shoes" he was about to release. But although he knew it was inevitable, Sam was reluctant to part with Elvis, and he kept raising the asking price for his contract.

Part of Sam's hesitancy was his dislike for Colonel Parker, but he finally gave Parker a one-month deadline to negotiate a deal. The price tag on Elvis's contract was $35,000, more than had ever been paid for a recording contract. Parker had been talking to several companies, but he focused most of his attention on RCA, which was about the only record company who might come up with that kind of money. But RCA had said $25,000 was as high as they would go. Parker began to put together a package deal with a music publisher, and kept sending telegrams to RCA to remind them that time was running out on the option. Parker was nothing if not a salesman, and in November 1955 RCA met the $35,000 asking price. Sam sold the contract and turned over to RCA all the tapes that Elvis had made for Sun Records.

During all this time, Elvis was in and out of Memphis, flying to performances now instead of driving. It was on one of his trips home between engagements that he and Dixie finally broke up. Elvis had not actually confessed that he had been unfaithful, but he didn't have to. With all of the one-night stands he had been playing, it was clear to Dixie that he must have had some other kind of one-night stands with the growing number of girls who literally threw themselves at him. But it wasn't just the sexual infidelity that proved the final breaking point. The life that he was leading was no kind of life to base a marriage and a future on. When they had talked about it in the quiet moments they had alone, Elvis agreed with her. But Elvis was having fewer and fewer of those quiet moments, and the dream that he was chasing was too tempting.

It was Dixie who told Elvis's mother and father that it was over. She and Gladys both cried, and in her heart Elvis's mother wished he would just stop now—take the money he had already made and settle down. But she knew that wasn't going to happen.

RCA wasted no time exploiting their new recording star. They immediately reissued all of the singles Elvis had made for Sun, and scheduled a recording session in their Nashville studio. Two days after his twenty-first birthday in January 1956, Elvis, Scotty, Bill, and D.J. all showed up in Nashville to cut their first record for their new label. Steve Sholes, the head of RCA's country western division and the man who had convinced his bosses back in New York to buy Elvis's contract, had sent Elvis a list of ten songs to consider for the first recording session and assembled a band to play behind the quartet.

Sholes was becoming increasingly nervous about

Elvis. Sam Phillips had just issued "Blue Suede Shoes" by Carl Perkins and "Folsom Prison Blues" by Johnny Cash, and both records were climbing the charts. A lot of executives at RCA headquarters in New York were beginning to wonder if Sholes hadn't bought the wrong singer. It didn't help when Elvis came into the studio with a new song he insisted would be his next release.

The song was one that Mae Axton, the Florida publicist for Colonel Parker, had brought to Elvis one night when they were both in Nashville for a DJ convention. It had been written by her and a friend. Elvis was polite as always, but he didn't really feel like hearing any songs. He was having fun at the convention.

Finally, he agreed to listen to it. He liked it immediately. "Hot dog, play it again, Mae," he said. He listened to it several times and by the end he had memorized the whole song. It was a song about a hotel, down at the end of Lonely Street, where the bellhop's tears kept flowing and the desk clerk was dressed in black.

When Elvis brought the song into his first RCA recording session in Nashville, there was considerable disappointment. Steve Sholes thought it was gloomy, not the upbeat sound he thought he was buying in Elvis Presley. But Elvis was adamant. He wanted "Heartbreak Hotel" to be his first RCA release.

When Sholes returned to New York, the RCA executives strongly recommended that Sholes not issue "Heartbreak Hotel." Sholes told his bosses that Elvis would be in New York soon, and they would find something better for his first RCA single then.

Meanwhile, the Colonel had been busy. Parker knew that he had to get Elvis national exposure, and the only way to do that was through television. By the mid-fifties most American homes had television sets. More people would see Elvis on one TV show than in a lifetime of Louisiana Hayride appearances. Parker arranged for Elvis to make four guest appearances on *Stage Show*, a CBS program on Saturday nights that was hosted by Jimmy and Tommy Dorsey, two of the biggest names from the Big Band era.

Elvis arrived in New York in January 1956 a few days before his debut TV appearance, and his first stop was at the RCA headquarters, where Sholes introduced their new recording star to the top brass. Whatever misgivings the RCA executives had about him couldn't have been helped when Elvis was introduced to the head of the company's record division. He had a gag buzzer hidden in the palm of his hand and gave the big boss a little shock as a practical joke when they shook hands.

Sholes was mortified and quickly steered Elvis to meet Anne Fulchino, a young go-getter from Boston who handled publicity for the pop-music department. Elvis also tried the buzzer trick when he shook hands with her. Fulchino looked him square in the eyes and told him, "Honey, that may work in Memphis, but it won't go over in New York." Elvis laughed, but always the quick study, he put the buzzer away.

Fulchino took him to lunch that day. As was often the case with Elvis, he was more comfortable opening up to women than to men. He confided to her that his goal was to make movies, to be the next James Dean. Over lunch, Fulchino decided that Elvis was a young man who knew what he wanted and would do whatever it took to get it. She returned to Sholes and excitedly told him, "We've found the guy we've been looking for."

Against the advice of his bosses, Sholes released

"Heartbreak Hotel" as Elvis's first single for RCA, on the day before his television debut. The Dorsey Brothers' TV program was produced by Jackie Gleason Enterprises and was a lead-in to Gleason's own popular comedy series *The Honeymooners*. The Dorsey Brothers had been big stars during the Swing era of the 1930s and '40s, but musical tastes had changed and *Stage Show* was not a success. Perhaps Gleason and the Dorseys were hoping to boost its ratings by bringing on this latest recording sensation, whoever he was.

The show was broadcast from CBS's Studio 50 on Broadway, between Fifty-third and Fifty-fourth Streets. It was a raw, rainy winter night. There were no screaming teenagers outside the theater, and only about half the seats inside were filled. In fact, a CBS publicist couldn't even give away the remaining tickets to passersby in Times Square. It was clear backstage that no one connected with the show had any idea what all the fuss was about. It wasn't even one of the Dorseys who introduced Elvis. Tommy Dorsey introduced Bill Randle, a New York disc jockey, as their "special guest," and it was Randle who introduced "a young fellow . . . who's going to make television history for you—Elvis Presley."

Elvis bounded out as he always had, nodded to Scotty and Bill and D.J., and launched into his version of "Shake, Rattle and Roll." It was a surprise choice. Both Sholes and Randle had expected Elvis to sing one of the songs he had recorded, even his new release of "Heartbreak Hotel." The Big Joe Turner classic was a song Elvis often performed in concert, but it was pure rhythm and blues. For Elvis, it made a statement that he was not just another country singer with a gimmick.

Elvis gave it everything he had. He jumped around the stage as much as he could within the confines of a television camera, and the studio audience didn't know whether to laugh or applaud.

During the week between the first of his four scheduled appearances, Elvis stayed in New York and spent several days in RCA's studios. Sholes was eager to get something on tape the RCA brass could get excited about. But nothing seemed to be working, and Sholes could sense that Elvis wasn't happy either. At one point, Sholes even called Sam Phillips back in Memphis and hinted that Sam should come to New York and work with Elvis as a sort of freelance producer. Sam, who bore Sholes no personal ill will over losing Elvis to RCA, assured Sholes that he had bought the right singer and advised him to just let Elvis do his own thing.

The second Dorsey show was an improvement, and Jackie Gleason Enterprises signed Elvis for an additional two appearances on *Stage Show*, making a total of six in all. By the time of his final appearance on *Stage Show*, Studio 50 was packed and Jimmy Dorsey was making the personal introductions. When Elvis announced he was going to sing his RCA single, "Heartbreak Hotel," the audience burst into screams.

Six weeks after it had been released, "Heartbreak Hotel" was near the top of the best-seller lists on three different charts—pop, country, and rhythm and blues. And his first album, titled *Elvis Presley*, which included Elvis's version of "Blue Suede Shoes," had been released and had sold nearly a million copies in less than a month. Even if the music industry didn't know how to classify Elvis, his music was spreading like wildfire. Steve Shoals finally knew he had bought the right singer.

On the morning after his final *Stage Show* appearance, Elvis flew to Los Angeles. The Colonel had set up a screen test for Elvis with Hal Wallis, one of Hollywood's top producers, whose films included *Casablanca, The Maltese Falcon*, and *Yankee Doodle Dandy*.

Wallis was about to start shooting *The Rainmaker* with Burt Lancaster and Katharine Hepburn. He had seen Elvis on TV and was struck by his good looks, not to mention the sales figures for his records and the frenzy swirling around him. He had even sent Elvis a copy of the screenplay so he could look it over before the screen test.

Elvis had told Colonel Parker that he didn't want to sing in movies. He wanted to play serious parts, like James Dean or Marlon Brando, two of his favorite actors. For the first part of his screen test, however, Elvis was given a toy guitar and told to lip-sync "Blue Suede Shoes." The idea was to see if the explosive energy Elvis created onstage and on television could come across on film. Allan Weiss, a screenwriter who was present, later wrote that "electricity bounced off the walls of the soundstage."

Wallis then had Elvis do a couple of scenes from *The Rainmaker*. Elvis had never even been in a high-school play, and his acting was stiff and wooden, but Weiss recalled that there was an "amateurish conviction" to the scenes. After the test, Wallis met with Elvis and asked him what kind of roles he wanted to play. Wallis came away from the meeting impressed with the polite young man, who clearly had a lot of raw energy, but did not immediately offer him a movie contract.

Another reason for Elvis's West Coast trip was to appear on *The Milton Berle Show*, which, unlike the Dorsey Brothers' *Stage Show*, was a top-rated program on television. Berle, or Uncle Miltie to his millions of fans, had risen from an old-time vaudeville trouper to become known as "Mr. Television."

The particular show Elvis appeared on was broadcast from aboard the *USS Hancock*, which was docked at the San Diego Naval Station. Elvis sang "Heartbreak Hotel" and was again greeted with screams and cheers, from an audience that was almost entirely made up of young sailors and their dates.

Elvis's appearance on *The Milton Berle Show* in 1956 is remembered mostly for a comedy skit in which Berle came onstage wearing a long-haired, Elvis-like wig and clown-sized blue suede shoes. He introduced himself as Melvin Presley, Elvis's unknown twin brother. Clearly Berle had no idea that Elvis had a twin brother who died at birth. They bantered back and forth, and Elvis joined in the routine, saying at one point, "I owe it all to you, Melvin." If Elvis felt any resentment over the skit he never showed it.

While Elvis was taking the West Coast by storm, the Colonel was working night and day to take advantage of all the press attention he was getting. Other TV shows began to line up to have Elvis make guest appearances. Hal Wallis decided that even if Elvis was not the next James Dean, he had a future in Hollywood, and he and the Colonel began negotiations on a movie contract. The rocket that was Elvis Presley had blasted off and was streaking toward the sky.

The Colonel also had the band booked into as many one-night stands as they could play. They were flying across the country from one show to the next, to the point that they didn't know what day it was or sometimes even what city they were in. And the concerts were becoming more and more unruly. There was nearly a riot at the San Diego Arena, and Elvis had to tell the crowd to go back to their seats or the show would end. At the end of the concert, there was such a mob of fans waiting outside that the musicians had to stay backstage for nearly an hour.

The unruliness of the fans became a big problem at concerts, and at the last Louisiana Hayride appearance, Horace Lee Logan made an announcement that other producers later repeated and which entered the popular culture as a sort of mantra: "Elvis has left the building."

The screaming from the girls got to be so loud that the music was virtually drowned out. The quartet couldn't even hear themselves onstage, and Scotty joked that they were the only band that was conducted by somebody's rear end, by which he meant they could only take their cues from Elvis's gyrations at the front of the stage. Elvis made a bet with Scotty that he could burp onstage and the girls would squeal. At the next show he did, and they did.

In every town they played, the local newspapers and radio stations wanted interviews, and Elvis always complied. The reporters wanted to know everything about him—his background, his family, the foods he liked. Some of the questions were more personal and he answered them all as truthfully as he could, although it didn't always help his image. A frequent question was about girls, whether there was anybody special, and were the rumors true that he had a different girl in every city. Elvis confided that he had been in love once but they had broken up soon after he started singing, and that he couldn't deny some of those rumors.

In fact, the girls were getting to be something of a problem. Elvis was often out half the night after a show, and he began to show up late for some of the concerts. When word of the problem reached the Colonel, he blamed Scotty and Bill for not keeping a better eye on his boy.

It was all happening so fast, and changing from day to day. Scotty and Bill had no illusions about their long-term future. They knew the Colonel would fire them in a minute if he thought Elvis would let him. Parker had already reprimanded and sent home from one tour Red West, Elvis's old high-school buddy who had been driving for them and was supposed to be Elvis's chaperone. But while the Colonel might snipe at Scotty and Bill and D.J., they knew Elvis would not listen to any suggestion that they be replaced.

Still, they knew the Colonel could be ruthless. He had bumped Bob Neal out of the picture by not renewing his contract and was now Elvis's lone manager, and he had bought out the band's contract with the Louisiana Hayride. Scotty, Bill, and D.J. knew that when their time came, the Colonel would dismiss them without blinking an eye.

In the middle of the tour, they got a call telling them to fly to Las Vegas. The Colonel booked them into a two-week gig at the New Frontier Hotel that would pay $7,500 a week. It was the first time they had played before an audience that was sitting down, and as Bill noted later, it was the first time in months they had been able to hear their own music.

The show, however, was close to a disaster. For one thing, it was a much older audience, and there were no squeals from the audience when Elvis swiveled his hips. The men wore suits and ties and the women were dressed more for an evening at a nightclub rather than a rock concert. They just sat and listened and then gave Elvis polite applause at the end.

But Vegas was like a vacation. They had to play only two twelve-minute shows a night, and the rest of the time they were free. Elvis caught several other shows around town. He saw Liberace and went backstage to tell the flamboyant pianist how much his mother loved him on TV. He also caught an act that featured a rendition of "Hound Dog," a song written by Jerry Leiber and Mike Stoller, two white teenagers who wrote songs for black R & B artists, and who would later write some songs for Elvis. "Hound Dog" had originally been recorded by Big Mama Thornton, and Elvis was determined to add it to his repertory.

They played out their two-week engagement and went home to Memphis. But Elvis had fallen in love with Vegas, partly because it was a city that never slept, and he told everybody he wanted to go back the first chance he got.

The reason for the trip back to Memphis was a big show at the Ellis Auditorium for the city's annual Cotton Carnival in May 1956. This time Elvis arrived for the show with a police escort and was mobbed by screaming fans as soon as he stepped out of the car. Gladys and Vernon were there, seated in a special box, and the emcee for the show was Bob Neal, his old manager. Elvis opened the show with "Heartbreak Hotel" and went through his usual repertory. As a finale, he launched into "Hound Dog." He had never sung it before, and the crowd went wild. As always when Elvis took over a song, he made it his own. Instead of a bouncy, bluesy tune, Elvis turned it into pure rock—faster, raucous, and uninhibited.

Elvis was home for almost a week, the longest he had been in Memphis at one time in nearly a year. Every day, scores of girls would gather outside his parents' house, and Gladys would have to go out and shoo them away. On the second day of his stay, he drove over to Dixie's house. It was the day of her graduation from high school, but when he suggested they go for a ride on his new motorcycle, she dropped everything and hopped on the bike. Elvis attended her graduation, but only as a friend. She had another date for the night. By the end of the week, Elvis was on his way back to California for a second appearance on *The Milton Berle Show* and some concerts on the West Coast.

The second show with Uncle Miltie lifted its ratings to the highest they had been all season, and Berle was clearly appreciative. "How about my boy?" Berle asked as he mussed Elvis's hair.

But the national exposure he was getting on his television appearances began to have a backlash. One of the biggest social issues of the 1950s was what was regarded as an increase in juvenile delinquency, and self-appointed moralists across the country were blaming the new rock-and-roll music in general, and Elvis in particular, as a major cause. Preachers began to denounce Elvis from the pulpits. One minister at a Baptist church in Florida said Elvis "achieved a new low in spiritual degeneracy." Some disc jockeys made public displays of breaking his records, and Ed Sullivan, who had the top-rated variety show on television, said he would not allow Elvis to appear on his program.

Elvis was already signed to make an appearance on *The Steve Allen Show* in New York, but Allen was so nervous about the criticism swirling around Elvis that he held a news conference to announce that Elvis would wear white tie and tails on the show, just to keep it clean. In an effort to turn the whole thing into a comedy routine, Allen even brought a basset hound onstage for Elvis to sing "Hound Dog" to. Elvis never complained at the time, but years later he would refer to the episode bitterly.

Elvis's appearance pushed *The Steve Allen Show* ahead of *The Ed Sullivan Show* in the ratings for the first time ever. Network executives may talk about not wanting to offend anybody, but ratings are ratings. After Elvis's guest shot with Steve Allen, Ed Sullivan changed his mind and signed Elvis for three appearances on his own show.

Although Elvis was always too polite to express any public bitterness at the criticism against him, the furor was beginning to get to him. He didn't mind so much those who said he couldn't sing. He knew he could sing. But it hurt him to know that preachers were denouncing him in church. He still gave interviews to just about anyone who asked for one, and he was as open and honest as he had always been. In a live television interview with the New York newspaper columnist Hy Gardner, he was asked how he felt about his critics. "Well," Elvis replied, "those people have a job to do and they do it." As for rock and roll, Elvis said: "I don't see how any type of music would have a bad influence on people when it's only music. . . . I mean, how would rock 'n' roll music make anyone rebel against their parents." Asked about all the negative press he was getting, Elvis responded: "Well, sir, you got to accept the bad along with the good. I've been getting some very good publicity . . . and I've been getting some bad publicity. I know that I'm doing the best that I can."

One of the few times Elvis ever showed anger was in defense of his fans. While on tour in Florida, he gave an interview to a reporter who was writing an article for *TV Guide*. The reporter quoted from other negative articles to get Elvis's reaction to them. One was from a Miami newspaper that referred to his fans as "two thousand idiots." Elvis flashed his irritation:

"Sir, those kids that come here and pay their money to see this show come to have a good time. I just don't see that he should call those people 'idiots.' Because they're somebody's kids. They're somebody's decent kids, probably, that was raised in a decent home, and he hasn't got any right to call those kids 'idiots.' If they want to pay their money to come out and jump around and scream and yell, it's their business. They'll grow up someday and grow out of that. While they're young let them have their fun."

CHAPTER SEVEN

ELVIS FLEW TO Hollywood to make his first movie in the middle of August 1956. Hal Wallis had told Colonel Parker he wouldn't have a script ready for Elvis until after the first of the year, so the Colonel signed him to do a movie at 20th Century Fox first.

The director had sent Elvis a copy of the screenplay, titled *The Reno Brothers*, and Elvis was so nervous about his movie debut he had learned the entire script by heart before he arrived—not just his part, but everybody else's as well. The Colonel had told Elvis he would have to sing some songs in the picture, but it was also a dramatic role.

It was a Civil War–era movie, and Elvis was to play the youngest of four brothers. He ends up marrying his

When Elvis first saw Graceland, a house his parents had seen while he was in Hollywood making a movie, he fell in love with it and bought it in a week in 1957.

oldest brother's girlfriend when he thinks his brother has been killed in the war. But the brother returns. The only thing that troubled Elvis about the script was that he was supposed to die at the end. He told the Colonel he didn't think it would be good for his fans if he died at the end of his first motion picture.

On the second day of shooting, Elvis began work on the sound track. The first song was the theme for the movie. It was an old Civil War tune called "Aura Lee," but with new words. It was a slow song, and there was concern how Elvis—the rock and roller whose music was anything but slow—would handle it. With only a pianist accompanying him, Elvis stood as though he were still a young boy in church and sang "Love Me Tender" for the first time. Everyone in the studio was stunned by the beauty of it. Elvis just shrugged and said: "I used to sing nothing but ballads. I love ballads."

Hollywood is a town where celebrity is the coin of the realm, and those who have it usually spend it freely. If any of the cast on the movie thought they might be in for a difficult time with a star who at that moment had more celebrity to throw around than anyone else in show business, they were in for a pleasant surprise.

Elvis was probably more starstruck than any tourist visiting the movie lot. He worked hard and made immediate friends with both cast and crew. He asked other cast members for advice, something actors are not reluctant to give. He had said he didn't want to take acting lessons because he wanted to be "natural." Mildred Dunnock, who appeared in the movie, said later that Elvis had two qualities as an actor that are essential: he listened to the other actors in scenes and he believed them.

In that September of 1956, Elvis interrupted shooting the movie to fly to New York for his first appearance on *The Ed Sullivan Show.* Elvis opened with "Don't Be Cruel," which had just been released, then handed his guitar to a stagehand and sang "Love Me Tender." The girls in the audience moaned and swooned, and it was clear they loved Elvis singing a ballad just as much as when he sang rock. The ratings were phenomenal. Over 87 percent of American households with televisions watched the show.

After work finished on the movie, which the producers had now decided to retitle *Love Me Tender*, Elvis returned to visit his parents and go with them to a special homecoming appearance in Tupelo that would include two concerts. It was a grand occasion, and Tupelo pulled out all the stops for a family that had left the town in the dead of night with all their possessions packed into a car just eight years earlier.

A huge banner across the main street read, "Tupelo Welcomes Elvis Presley Home." It was an emotional day for Gladys and Vernon. Gladys later told a friend, "It made me feel bad to go back there like that and remember how poor we was." Even Elvis couldn't resist one crack about the difference in the situation. When he showed up at the fairgrounds, he said it was the first time he had ever gone through the main gate; he had always had to climb the fence to get in when he lived there. The concerts were sold out, with some fifty thousand people attending them.

A few weeks later, Elvis went to New York for his second Ed Sullivan appearance. The show was either a great success or an outrageous demonstration of vulgarity, depending on how one felt about Elvis and his movements onstage. It certainly fueled the controversy that now followed him everywhere he went. It had gotten to the point that he couldn't even drive around Memphis anymore without creating a scene.

If he left his Cadillac on the street for even a short period of time, he would return to find it covered with love notes, addresses, and telephone numbers written in lipstick.

Love Me Tender opened just before Thanksgiving of 1956. In a last-minute concession to his fans, many of whom had been carrying placards pleading for Elvis not to die in the film, the director shot a new ending for the movie. It consisted of Elvis, alive and superimposed over the shot of his character dying, singing "Love Me Tender." The reviews were predictably condescending, but an estimated fifteen hundred teenagers stood in line for the first screening in New York City at eight A.M.

In January 1957, just as Elvis turned twenty-two and before he returned to Hollywood for his next movie, he made his last appearance on *The Ed Sullivan Show*. There had been a new round of attacks on Elvis for his hip-swiveling gyrations, and Sullivan instructed his cameramen to frame him only from the waist up. For his final number, as a way of taking the wind out of the moral crusaders' sails, Elvis sang the old spiritual "Peace in the Valley."

At the end of the show, as the screams were still

echoing around the theater, Sullivan came out and silenced the audience. "I wanted to say to Elvis Presley and the country that this is a real decent, fine boy, and wherever you go, Elvis, we want to say that we've never had a pleasanter experience on our show with a big name than we've had with you. Let's have a tremendous hand for a very nice person."

Despite Sullivan's personal endorsement, Colonel Parker had decided that enough was enough. The Colonel had used television to make Elvis a household name, but the criticism was now becoming too virulent and too personal. It had even reached Congress where there were hearings on the influence of rock and roll on juvenile delinquency. Both the Colonel and Hal Wallis, who was lining up more movies for Elvis, had long-range plans to build his career into something that would last longer than rock and roll. While they were very different personalities, the Colonel and Wallis were both shrewd businessmen. The Colonel began to ease Elvis out of having so many concert dates, and Wallis planned to make him a star of the kind of movies you could take the family to.

Perhaps taking a cue from Elvis's first movie, Wallis decided to rename his next film after the song that would be the main theme, a ballad that had been written especially for the movie, called "Loving You."

The filming was interspersed with some recording sessions for RCA. Steve Shoals flew out from New York, and Scotty, Bill, and D.J. came in from Memphis, and when Elvis had any free time from the movie set, he was in the recording studio. They cut the songs for the movie sound track and then did some religious numbers, including "Peace in the Valley" and "Take My Hand, Precious Lord."

During the shooting, Elvis brought his parents out to Los Angeles for a visit. The trip was delayed briefly because Gladys had become ill and went into the hospital for a series of tests. But the doctors found nothing specifically wrong, and she and Vernon spent about a month in Los Angeles. Elvis showed them around town and got them tickets to Tennessee Ernie Ford's television show, one of their favorites. Tennessee Ernie even introduced them in the audience. They visited the movie set frequently, and the director put them in the final scene, in which the character Elvis played sings to a live television audience.

When they got home, Gladys told all her friends she was amazed at how Hollywood was treating Elvis.

"There's somebody to comb his hair for him, and even a man to help him get dressed and another man to ask him if he's ready to work."

By the time Elvis arrived back in Memphis in March, Gladys and Vernon had another surprise for him. They had been looking at houses, and the real-estate agent had found one they thought he would love. Elvis went to look at it the day after he got home.

The house was a colonial that had been built in 1939 as a country home for an old Memphis family, about eight miles south of the city. It was on eighteen acres of land, full of oak trees, all that was left of what had once been a five-hundred-acre farm. It had eighteen rooms and had been named for an elderly member of the original family—Aunt Grace.

Elvis fell in love with Graceland immediately and agreed to pay the asking price on the spot. Within a week, Elvis had bought Graceland for a total of about $102,000. He was full of plans for the house and called in architects and decorators. He wanted the most beautiful bedroom in Memphis for his mother, and he wanted a real soda fountain installed in the den. He wanted a swimming pool and big locking gates with a music motif, so there wouldn't be hundreds of fans waiting on the driveway every morning when he woke up. And he also wanted a chicken coop built, because Gladys had said she wanted to raise some chickens.

For the first time, Elvis's life began to take on a sort of routine. He would travel to Hollywood to make a movie, then return home to Memphis. The Colonel would organize occasional concert tours, but they would be mostly big-city venues for brief periods—a week or ten days. When he was in Hollywood, he took over the penthouse at the Beverly Wilshire Hotel. When he was in Memphis he was at Graceland.

From the start of his Hollywood career, Elvis developed a habit of bringing along friends or relatives to keep him company. His cousin Gene Smith had gone with him for his first movie. For *Jailhouse Rock*, he got his friend George Klein to come along. Over the months, other friends and relatives from Memphis like Junior Smith, another cousin, and Red West joined him. As the number of people invited along for the ride increased, Elvis found jobs for most of them—as driver, personal assistant, or just general gofer—and put them on the payroll. With his new friends in Los

Angeles, Elvis soon had a complete entourage going back and forth with him between Memphis and Hollywood.

Similarly, a pattern developed with his parade of girlfriends. If he met a girl he wanted to see again, he would invite her to Graceland. He would take her on a tour that included Humes High School, the Lauderdale Courts, the Sun Records studio, Daddy-O Dewey Phillips's radio program, Crown Electric where he had driven a truck, the roller rink, the fairgrounds, and maybe a ride on his new motorcycle.

Sometimes these visits dangerously overlapped. Once when one of his more serious girlfriends, June Juanico, was in town, he announced that Natalie Wood, a beautiful actress he had met through a Hollywood friend named Nick Adams, was arriving. June, who had dated Elvis all one summer and had even joined him on one of his tours, went home to Mississippi in a huff.

All the girls who came through Memphis were warmly welcomed by Gladys, who treated them all like they were already members of the family. The list of women Elvis dated grew week by week. He asked out almost every pretty girl he met, and the gossip columns had him engaged to most of them.

By this time, Elvis had become a victim of his own success. He could no longer go outside his house without creating a near riot. When he wanted to go to the movies he had to rent the entire theater. When he wanted to go to a restaurant, he had to have a private room. If Elvis could not go out and have fun, the fun had to come to Elvis.

Elvis's suite at the Beverly Wilshire in Hollywood and the guest rooms at Graceland became open houses where some sort of nonstop party was always in progress. His world was becoming more and more confined to the hotel, the movie studio, and his home in Memphis. As his seclusion grew, and the number of new faces in the Presley group photo kept increasing, jealousies arose between the Memphis crew, who had become known as the Memphis Mafia, and the Hollywood crowd.

There were also rifts with some of his oldest friends. Dewey Phillips visited at one point, and his cornpone antics slightly embarrassed Elvis in front of his new Hollywood friends. But what caused a real falling-out between them came when Elvis played Dewey a dub of "Teddy Bear," a new single for RCA. When he left, Dewey sneaked a copy of the song into his luggage and played it on his radio show as soon as he got back to Memphis. RCA was furious, and Elvis felt Dewey had betrayed him.

The situation with Scotty and Bill, who were upset because they were still on retainers and a salary, reached a climax on a trip to Hollywood in September 1957 to record a Christmas album for RCA. The musicians had been promised studio time to record some instrumentals on their own after the album was finished, but when Elvis left the studio, they were told the session was over. It was the final straw for Scotty and Bill, and they wrote a letter of resignation and sent it to Elvis's hotel. D.J., who had always been paid a straight fee, did not sign it.

Elvis was angry and sad. When he got back to Memphis, he called Scotty and offered him and Bill a raise. But then Scotty gave an interview in which he accused Elvis of not keeping his word. Elvis felt betrayed even further and issued his own statement wishing Scotty and Bill good luck in the future.

Elvis stopped by Sun Records to see Sam Phillips, but things weren't the same there either. Marion Keisker and Sam had had a big argument and she had quit. He went to see Daddy-O Dewey, and they sort of made up, but he still felt he could no longer trust the disc jockey. Finally, he called Scotty and they worked out a deal. But he felt his life had become a train hurtling out of control, and he didn't know how to stop it.

Just a week before Christmas of 1957, the twenty-two-year-old Elvis had a call from his local draft board telling him that his induction notice had arrived. It was just after the Korean War and before the Vietnam War, but there was still a mandatory draft, and all able-bodied American men had to fulfill their military service. Colonel Parker tried all of his contacts to try to get around it, but the army is the army, and Elvis didn't want his fans to think he was shirking his duty. The next day, Elvis went by the draft board and got the letter. He opened it, and the familiar word "Greetings" stared back at him. All too soon, he would be "Private Presley."

CHAPTER EIGHT

IN THE END, Elvis got a two-month deferment in order to make his next movie, *King Creole*, which had been scheduled to begin shooting early in 1958. The head of Paramount Studios had written the draft board pleading financial hardship on the basis that they would lose all of the money they had already spent on preproduction costs if Elvis were unable to make the picture. The draft board was sympathetic but needed the request from Private Presley himself. Elvis duly wrote, and the deferment was granted.

Steve Sholes flew out to try to get some songs on tape that RCA could release while Elvis was in uniform, and between shooting the movie and recording for RCA, he had a busy two months. He returned to Memphis for a few days before reporting for duty, then, on the appointed morning, Elvis arrived at the draft board office at 6:35 A.M., accompanied by a caravan of cars packed with friends and relatives. It was drizzling rain, and dozens of photographers and reporters were on hand.

"If I seem nervous," Elvis said, "it's because I am." He went on to tell the reporters that he thought the army would be a great experience and he didn't want to be treated differently than anybody else.

A short time later, the inductees were taken to a nearby veteran's hospital for a physical, and then packed on buses to be driven to Fort Chaffee, Arkansas. There he got his G.I. haircut, one of the most photographed haircuts in barbering history. "Hair today, gone tomorrow," Elvis joked as his long locks fell away. He was issued an olive drab uniform, and he was assigned to a unit at Fort Hood, Texas—the Second Armored Division, the famous "Hell on Wheels" outfit of General George Patton during World War II.

For the first few days, some of the other guys in his company gave him some grief. They might, for example, ask him if he missed his teddy bears. But when they saw Elvis could take a joke, he quickly became accepted. His sergeant, Bill Norwood, saw that he was homesick, and he let Elvis use the phone in his house to make calls to his mother. He won a marksman's medal with his rifle and a sharpshooter's prize with his pistol and even pulled KP duty. He was training to be a tank gunner, and he placed third in his company.

The Colonel, who always read the fine print, discovered an army regulation that permitted servicemen to live off base if they had dependents living nearby. Gladys and Vernon could certainly count as dependents. Elvis consulted Sergeant Norwood, who told him he would qualify for off-base living once basic training was completed.

Gladys and Vernon packed up and moved to Killeen, the Texas town next to Fort Hood, within days. Elvis rented a house in the middle of town, and Killeen became a long-distance extension of Graceland. Fans poured into the town, and there was the usual flow of visitors from Memphis and Hollywood. Gladys once again welcomed them all, but after about a month in Killeen, she began to feel unwell. She lost color, felt tired, and was unable to eat. She called her doctor in Memphis and asked him to come down to Texas, but in the end she decided to return home.

Elvis's parents left Killeen by train on a Friday, and the next day her physician, Dr. Charles Clarke, admitted Gladys to the hospital. Dr. Clarke could not figure out what was wrong with her. She had a liver problem, but it wasn't hepatitis or jaundice. He called in specialists, but no one could diagnose the trouble. By Monday, she hadn't improved and Dr. Clarke knew it was serious. He called Elvis and suggested he should come home.

Elvis had just begun six weeks' training with his tank crew, and his commanding officer at the base was reluctant to let him leave, since it would look like he was giving Elvis special privileges. Dr. Clarke, who had served five years in the army, pointed out to the commanding officer how bad it would look if he denied any serviceman leave to visit his gravely ill mother. The next day Elvis was on a plane to Memphis.

He went straight from the airport to the hospital, and Gladys perked up just seeing him. Elvis thought she didn't look as bad as he had feared. He came back the next morning and again in the afternoon and stayed until almost midnight, promising to return the first thing the next morning. It was about three thirty A.M. when the telephone rang.

"I knew what it was before I answered the telephone," Elvis said later. Vernon, who had been sleeping on a cot in Gladys's room, was awakened by the sound of Gladys gasping for breath. They rang for the doctor, but she died before he could arrive. As soon as Elvis reached the hospital, he fell on his knees beside her bed and began to wail.

Elvis was inconsolable in his grief. For the next few days, Elvis and Vernon clung to each other. When reporters arrived at Graceland later that morning, they saw Elvis and his father sitting alone on the front steps of the house, their arms around each other, rocking gently and sobbing. They were oblivious to anything else.

On the morning of the funeral, August 14, 1958, over three thousand people visited the Memphis Funeral Home. Sixty-five policemen were on hand to keep order. When Elvis arrived for the service, he had to be helped from the limousine. Just before the service was to begin, Dixie arrived. Now married and a mother herself, she went over to the alcove in the chapel that was reserved for family. When he saw her, Elvis leapt up and said, "Look, Dad, here's Dixie." He hugged her and cried and asked her to come to Graceland that night.

Reverend Hamill preached the service, and the Blackwood Brothers, who had been Gladys's favorite

The death of Elvis's mother, Gladys, shattered Elvis and his father, Vernon, and they shared their grief on the steps of Graceland.

gospel group, sang. When they sang the hymn "Precious Mem'ries," Elvis began to sob, "Oh, Dad, no, no, no."

The scene at the cemetery was just as wrenching. When the graveside service was finished, Elvis leaned over the casket and cried "Good-bye, darling, good-bye. I love you so much." Friends had to half drag him back to the car. "Oh, God," he said as he left, "everything I have is gone."

Dixie drove by Graceland that night, but the house looked like a mob scene. There were twenty or thirty cars in the driveway, and the grounds were filled with people. She had her hair in rollers, and she was wearing shorts. She did not want to intrude, so she told the guard at the gate to send a message to Elvis that Dixie had stopped by and would come back the next night. Before she could leave, however, one of Elvis's cousins came up and said Elvis was waiting for her at the house and had been asking for her all night. He escorted her through the crowd, and Elvis was waiting to meet her at the front door.

When they went inside, the only other person she saw was his grandmother. Dixie asked where everybody was, since there were so many cars out in the driveway. "I told them to get lost," Elvis said.

Dixie and Elvis spent the evening going over old times. They sang some songs and reminisced, and Elvis told her he wished he could just walk away from this life and go back. "Why don't you?" Dixie asked. "You've done what you wanted to do."

Elvis shook his head. "It's too late for that," he said. "There are too many people. There are too many people that depend on me. I'm in too far to get out."

Elvis asked Dixie to come back the next night, and she did. But this time the house was filled with people, and Dixie realized what Elvis meant. She only stayed a short time. It was the last time Dixie saw him.

When he returned to Fort Hood, Elvis had only a few weeks left of his basic training before he was scheduled to ship out to Germany. Elvis and his unit arrived by train at the old Brooklyn Army Terminal in New York to find that Colonel Parker had organized a reception worthy of the circus carny he once was. A crowd of over one hundred reporters and photographers were waiting, along with the top executives from RCA, his father and grandmother, and hundreds of fans. Elvis held a news conference, posed for pictures, and then, as he walked up the gangway to the ship, a band played "Hound Dog" and "Don't Be Cruel." Elvis turned, rotated his shoulder, snapped his fingers, and swiveled his hips. The fans squealed, and Elvis smiled and waved good-bye.

As it turned out, Elvis's army life in Germany wasn't all that different from his life in Killeen, Graceland, or even Hollywood. His father, grandmother, and several friends all came with him. He again got permission to live off base, and he rented a house at Goethestrasse 14, in Bad Nauheim, a twenty-minute drive from the base. His grandmother, Minnie Presley, whom he called Dodger, made him home-cooked meals.

But as much as life seemed the same, there were differences, too. Elvis had become more demanding of his friends' attention. He insisted, for example, that everyone get up and have breakfast with him at five thirty A.M. before he left for the base. He was also quicker to show his displeasure, often blowing up at any perceived slight. He never wanted to go to bed, and he expected everyone to stay up with him. It was as though he feared his life was slipping away from him, and he didn't want to miss a minute of it.

But the double life of soldier and party boy finally caught up with him. While he was on maneuvers one week, he couldn't stay awake. A sergeant gave him a little bottle of pills and told Elvis they would pump him back up with all the energy he needed. The sergeant assured Elvis the pills were completely harmless.

Elvis became an instant believer in amphetamines. He would take one any time he began to feel tired. Then he would be able to stay up all night. The pills made him feel as though everything was all right. But everything wasn't all right, of course. What the sergeant didn't tell Elvis was that amphetamines can also increase irritability and create heart irregularities, and they are addictive.

And Elvis had a lot that was irritating him. The thing that most upset him was that his father had started seeing a woman named Dee Stanley, who was the wife of a master sergeant stationed in Frankfurt and the mother of three children. Elvis felt Vernon's romance with Dee was not only improper, but it was too soon after his mother's death.

A happier event during his time in Germany came one night when an airman named Currie Grant brought a girl he knew to a party at Elvis's house. When they came in, Elvis stood up and went to greet her. "Hi, I'm Elvis Presley," he said. The girl was speechless. Grant introduced her, "This is Priscilla Beaulieu."

Elvis was smitten from the start. Priscilla was very attractive—dark hair, a button nose, and, like Elvis, sexy eyes and pouty lips—but she also was clearly very young. Elvis asked her what grade she was in at school—a junior or a senior in high school? "Ninth," she replied. "Ninth what?" he asked. "Grade," she said.

Despite later newspaper reports that she was older, Priscilla Beaulieu was just fourteen when she met the twenty-four-year-old Elvis. She was the stepdaughter of an air force captain, who had raised her with her mother from the time she was an infant. Her real father had been a navy pilot who had died in an airplane crash.

From the moment of their introduction that first night, Elvis gave Priscilla his full attention. He played the piano and sang for her and took her to the kitchen to meet Dodger, his grandmother. When she had to leave, he asked her back.

By the fourth date, Captain Beaulieu insisted on meeting Mr. Presley, so Elvis got his father to go with him. The captain wasted no time in asking why Elvis, who had girls throwing themselves at him, wanted to see his daughter. As Priscilla later recalled, Elvis replied: “Well, sir, I happen to be very fond of her. I guess you might say I need someone to talk to. You don’t have to worry about her, Captain. I’ll take good care of her.”

Elvis’s attentions to Priscilla fit into a pattern he had developed with all young women he really cared about—going all the way back to Dixie. He liked to kiss and cuddle, and he felt he could open his heart to them. But he was adamant about not going all the way. For the rest of his time in Germany, Elvis saw Priscilla as often as he could. When they were alone, he would confide to her his fears that nobody would remember him when he got out of the army.

By the end, Elvis had earned his sergeant’s stripes, and he had been accepted as one of the guys. Still, he was excited and anxious about returning home. The Colonel had made big plans for his return—a TV special with Frank Sinatra, some recording sessions, and more movies. If he was nervous about his popularity, the crowds that turned out in Germany to send him off should have reassured him. At the airport, Priscilla was prevented from having a last good-bye by a group of military policemen, but the reporters noticed her, and her picture was in the next day's papers under the caption, "The Girl He Left Behind."

Colonel Parker had organized a homecoming that included a whistle-stop train ride back to Memphis with crowds in every town they went through. Elvis had been in the army for two years, but the fans who turned out to greet him in March 1960 cheered him as though he were a savior returned to their midst.

Elvis was back at Graceland for only two weeks before he had to leave again for a recording session in Nashville and then to Miami to tape the Frank Sinatra special that was billed as a welcome home party for Elvis. After that, he headed to Los Angeles to start work on *G.I. Blues*.

If it appeared on the surface that he had picked up his life where he left off, Elvis himself knew that nothing was quite the same. He still made movies and records, with some r-and-r at Graceland sandwiched in between. And he still had the usual cast of characters in and out of his entourage wherever he went. It was work during the day and play at night, all made possible by a steady diet of those little pills. But the work was monotonous, the partying more forced, and his temper tantrums at various members of his posse more frequent.

It was not the same old Elvis. At recording sessions, he still showed the professionalism that had been his trademark, but the other musicians noticed that a spark was gone. Even the movies that he was now making were different. In the earlier roles, Elvis had been cast as a kind of youthful rebel, and there was a freshness and sincerity to his work that was now missing. In the new scripts, the situations did not seem real to him, and his lack of interest in the material showed up on the screen.

He was now spending so much time in Hollywood that he rented a house there. His world became even more insular, and he was seldom outside the company of the gang. The circle of friends changed from time to time as one or another of his cronies fell out of favor, only to be accepted back when Elvis's mood would swing the other way. It was almost impossible for him to go out in public. Once he took Anita Wood, a former beauty queen who was the one serious girlfriend to bridge the years before and after the army, to church in Memphis, but they had to leave because the crush of fans made a worship service impossible.

The only place he could go about with relative freedom anymore was Las Vegas, a wide-open city where slot machines trumped celebrities and where even the biggest stars dimmed in a skyline that blazed neon. In fact, he sometimes went to Las Vegas between his movie jobs rather than return to Graceland, because things were not the same there either.

Vernon was still seeing Dee, who by now had left her husband, and in the summer of 1960 they were married. Elvis was crushed by the turn of events, but he always spoke politely of his stepmother. And he refused to criticize Vernon. In an interview in *The Memphis Press-Scimitar* shortly after the wedding, Elvis said: "He is my father and he's all I got left in the world. He stood by me all these years and sacrificed things he wanted so that I could have clothes and lunch money to go to school. I'll stand by him now—right or wrong."

Vernon and Dee moved into Graceland, and it was one of the reasons Elvis no longer looked forward to returning there.

The Colonel arranged for him to appear at two benefit concerts—one in Memphis and another in Hawaii, where Elvis was heading to film *Blue Hawaii*. The shows, especially the one in Honolulu, caught a glimpse of the old Elvis, laughing and digging the music and feeding off the fans. But the show in Hawaii was his last public concert for eight years.

During the summer of 1962, Elvis finally convinced Captain Beaulieu to let Priscilla come visit him in Los Angeles. Elvis and Priscilla had kept up during the two years since he had left the army by talking on the phone and corresponding. When the captain agreed to let her visit, he set a list of conditions that Elvis first had to meet, including finding a place for her to stay where she would be well chaperoned. Elvis enlisted the help of a car dealer from whom he was buying a mobile home, who agreed to let Priscilla stay with his family, although Elvis had no intention of her actually spending much time there.

When she arrived in June, Priscilla was nervous. She hadn't seen Elvis in two years, and she wasn't sure how he would react to her. One of Elvis's friends picked her up at the airport and drove her straight to the house. When she walked in, the room was full of people and Elvis was playing pool. When he saw her, Elvis threw down his pool cue and came to her and kissed her in front of all the others. That was certainly different from Germany, when he had never touched her until they were alone. But she spent the rest of her first evening there watching Elvis play king for the entourage.

It was only later, when they were alone, that she saw the old Elvis she had known in Germany. She stayed for two weeks, and Elvis showed her the sights of Hollywood, then drove her to Las Vegas. She wrote several postcards to her mother and stepfather, and Elvis got a friend to mail one each day so her parents would think she was still in Los Angeles. Priscilla had trouble getting used to the hours Elvis kept, staying up most of the night and sleeping a few hours during the day, but Elvis gave her some amphetamines to keep her going.

When Priscilla left, Elvis returned to Memphis. As soon as he arrived, Anita Wood could tell that something was different. Anita was the original Girl He Left Behind when Elvis went into the army, and he had kept her on a string ever since. Anita had no illusions about all the other girls Elvis saw—his co-stars in movies and the showgirls who were in and out of his nonstop parties. After all, there were pictures in the papers and magazines. But Elvis had always told her the other girls meant nothing to him.

This time, with all the instincts that only a jilted lover can have, Anita knew it was over. She had believed that she and Elvis would marry some day, and she wanted to settle down and have a family. When she learned from all the whispered conversations and secret phone calls that the "girl from Germany" had been over for a visit, she decided she had had enough. She packed her bags and told Elvis she was leaving. They both cried. Anita was the last of Elvis's girls his mother had known, and Gladys had liked Anita a lot. But Elvis did not try to stop her from going.

CHAPTER NINE

NO SOONER HAD Priscilla returned to Germany than Elvis began working on a plan to have her come spend her Christmas holidays with him in Memphis. He again had to convince Captain Beaulieu that everything was proper. This time he promised that Priscilla would stay with his father and stepmother, who by now had moved out of Graceland into their own home nearby. At the end of the two weeks, Elvis called her stepfather to ask if she could extend her stay, but the captain insisted she return home.

But Elvis was by now unaccustomed to not having his way. He launched a campaign for Priscilla to move to Memphis. This time Elvis had a strong ally in Priscilla. She informed her parents that she was now seventeen, no longer a child, and made clear she would be a rebel with a cause if they did not let her go. For his part, Elvis promised that she would enroll in school in Memphis, that she would live with Vernon and Dee, and that she would always be chaperoned.

In the end, her parents gave up. In March 1963, Captain Beaulieu and Priscilla flew first to Los Angeles, where Elvis was working on another movie, to finalize the agreement, then to Memphis where the captain helped get her enrolled in school and settled into Vernon and Dee's house. By the time Elvis was home again after finishing the movie, Priscilla already had moved into Graceland.

For the next few months, Elvis and Priscilla played house. They were constantly together, even if they weren't often alone. Elvis's entourage seemed to trail behind them everywhere they went. Elvis bought her a new red sports car so Vernon wouldn't have to drive her to school every day. But it was a different life from any Priscilla had ever imagined. They were always surrounded by either Elvis's gang of friends and relations or his fans. When Priscilla graduated from high school, Elvis had to wait outside in the car because his presence might interrupt the commencement ceremonies.

Elvis returned to Hollywood in the summer for

his next movie, *Viva Las Vegas*. His co-star was the sexy actress Ann-Margret, and the chemistry between them began to bubble from the moment they met on the set. Before long they were an item in all the gossip columns in newspapers. Unlike Anita, Priscilla was not the kind of girl to turn a blind eye to Elvis's romances, and when he returned to Memphis after the filming, she confronted him. As he always had, Elvis tried to play down the relationship, assuring Priscilla that Ann-Margret was just another starlet.

When Elvis returned to Hollywood to start his next movie, however, the stories of a romance persisted, and Ann-Margret gave an interview in London in which she said she was going steady with Elvis and was in love with him, and even hinted at possible marriage. Priscilla and Elvis both exploded, though for different reasons, and Elvis promised Priscilla that he would never see Ann-Margret again. It wasn't quite true. They were together in Hollywood the day President Kennedy was assassinated in Dallas, in November 1963, and spent the weekend together watching television. As with all his flings with his co-stars, however, the one with Ann-Margret eventually cooled.

But with each new movie, Elvis seemed more subdued and defeated. He also began to have doubts about the decisions Colonel Parker was making. The Colonel was always mindful of the bottom line. In making *Viva Las Vegas* the producers had gone over budget, which cut into Elvis's—and the Colonel's—profits. For Elvis's next movies, the Colonel insisted on hiring directors who could keep costs down, and who could shoot a movie in two or three weeks instead of two or three months.

As far as the Colonel was concerned, the formula they had was working just fine. Elvis would record a sound track for a movie and RCA would issue records from it. The movie would help record sales, and the record would help the movie at the box office.

For Elvis, the routine was a rut. Elvis was not dumb. He knew he had not had a gold record in over two years, and he could work up little passion for the songs he had to sing in the movies. He was no longer giving concerts, and the cardboard characters he had to play in the movies—he made thirty-three films during his career—were boring.

The dissatisfaction with his work was a two-way

street. Hal Wallis wrote to the Colonel at the end of 1963 that Elvis had looked fat in his latest movie and that his by-now dyed black hair looked like a wig. Elvis had always fought a battle with his weight—his love of such food as peanut-butter-and-banana sandwiches and ham with cream potatoes and red-eye gravy was famous—and he was taking diet pills in addition to the uppers and downers with which he regulated his life.

Even the Colonel was becoming concerned. The latest movies were not making as much money as the early ones, and record sales were falling. Elvis still had his fans, but many of his original fans were now married with children, a station wagon, and a mortgage. Teenagers were now screaming for the Beatles.

Elvis took up spirituality for a while. A guru hairdresser named Larry Geller joined the circle in 1964 for a time, and fed Elvis a diet of transcendental books. Later, Elvis got into horses and bought so many that in 1967 he purchased a 160-acre ranch in Mississippi, which he named the "Flying Circle G" in memory of his mother, just to stable them all. He also started lessons in karate, which he had first learned in the army.

Elvis and Priscilla were finally married on May 1, 1967. Elvis had proposed, on his knees, the previous Christmas, but they had not set a date. After he finished another movie at the end of April, Elvis and Priscilla flew to Las Vegas for a wedding ceremony in a hotel—a ceremony so private that even some of Elvis's oldest friends were not invited.

After a weekend in Palm Springs, the newlyweds flew home to Graceland. Priscilla, at twenty-one and now the lady of the house, took charge. She also decided they would buy a house in Los Angeles rather than rent one, a move that would limit the access of some of the wilder members of Elvis's posse. To do that, they had to sell the ranch and most of the horses. The Colonel had just weeks earlier warned Elvis that he had to start watching his spending, and some of the entourage were cut from the payroll.

Shortly before they returned to California for the next movie, Priscilla learned that she was pregnant. If she was somewhat ambivalent about it happening so soon after their marriage, Elvis was elated. In an interview years later, Priscilla recalled: "For the first year I truly wanted to be alone with Elvis, without any responsibilities or obligations. I expected him to [have] the same mixed reactions, but he was ecstatic." Elvis's only regret was that Gladys had not lived long enough to see the grandchild she so dearly wanted.

Lisa Marie Presley was born on February 1, 1968, nine months to the day after her parents married, and Elvis spent the nine hours of Priscilla's labor pacing the floor of the hospital like any other expectant father. For the next two weeks, Elvis kept picking her up from her crib so much, Priscilla had to tell him to leave her alone. "She's a little miracle," he would tell everyone who came to call.

In an effort to jump-start a career that had grown stagnant, the Colonel had been working on a deal with NBC for an Elvis Presley Christmas special that year. It would be Elvis's first television appearance in eight years. Elvis agreed to do it, but without enthusiasm.

The special was to be shot that summer, and NBC hired a young director named Steve Binder to put together the show. The Colonel's idea had been to have an hour of Elvis singing Christmas songs, but Binder wanted the thirty-three-year-old Elvis to make a statement to the world about who he really was. He came up with an idea to build the show around *The Blue*

With the birth of their daughter, Lisa Marie, Elvis and Priscilla enjoyed one of the happiest periods of their life together.

Bird, a play about a boy who travels the world in search of fame and fortune only to find true happiness is back home. The central musical theme would be Jerry Reed's "Guitar Man." Binder was nervous when he presented the idea to Elvis and urged him to suggest any changes. Elvis listened to the plan and said, "No, I like it all."

The show ran into problems when the music producer Parker had insisted on hiring never came up with any arrangements. If Binder fired him, he was afraid Elvis would walk out. But Elvis just nodded when Binder told him and said, "Do what you have to do." Binder turned to Billy Goldenberg, a Broadway conductor who was not a big fan of rock and roll. Binder had no idea how he and Elvis were going to get along.

As Goldenberg later recounted, the first time he walked into the studio, Elvis was sitting at a piano playing the opening bars of Beethoven's "Moonlight Sonata." Elvis, who over the course of his music career had learned to play the piano as well as the guitar, asked him if he knew it, and Goldenberg said he did. Elvis asked him what came next, so Goldenberg sat beside him at the piano and showed him the next few bars. Every evening, Goldenberg would spend time teaching Elvis more of the sonata. But if one of the gang should walk in, Elvis would close the lid of the piano and pick up his guitar.

As rehearsals began, Elvis began to show more interest in the project. He even liked the black leather jumpsuit the costume designer came up with. The show was to include segments taped before a live audience to represent Elvis's early career. Binder even brought in Scotty Moore and D.J. Fontana, his original guitarist and drummer, to appear on it. Bill Black, the bass player, had died a couple of years earlier from a brain tumor at the age of thirty-nine.

When the time came to tape the live performance, however, Elvis became very nervous and even told Binder he couldn't go on. The format was for Elvis and the musicians to sit on a small, square stage sort of like a boxing ring with the audience surrounding them. Elvis appeared uneasy at the beginning, and sang some humorous lyrics to "Love Me Tender" to break the tension. But once the audience got involved, Elvis threw himself into the songs and gave them everything he had. At one point he asked for a strap for his guitar so he could stand up and sing. When no one could find one, he stood up anyway and sang with his guitar propped on one knee. He was bathed in sweat by the end, laughing, joking, and clearly loving what he was doing more than he had in years.

After the taping was over, Elvis went to his dressing room and told one of the guys he wanted to see the Colonel. When Parker came in, Elvis told him: "I want to tour again. I want to go out and work with a live audience."

The finale for the show was a song Binder had Earl Brown write especially for it called "If I Can Dream." The Colonel kept insisting on some kind of Christmas song at the end, but when Binder played the new song for him, Elvis listened to it several times, and insisted on doing it.

It had been only a few months since the Reverend Dr. Martin Luther King Jr. had been assassinated in Memphis, and this song about a world where all people walk hand in hand echoed King's famous "I have a dream" speech. Elvis, standing alone onstage in a white double-breasted suit, unleashed all of his passion and emotion in the song, swinging his right hand like a pendulum, and almost shouting the plea in the song's final lines to let the dream come true right now.

When the show aired in December 1968, it became as much a part of TV history as Elvis's first appearance over a decade earlier. Elvis's Christmas special was the number one show of the season. And when the single of "If I Can Dream" was released, shortly before the album sound track of the TV show, it became Elvis's biggest-selling record in four years. Peter Guralnick, who as a young man was more a fan of the Beatles and the Rolling Stones than of Elvis, reviewed the show for a Boston newspaper, and later wrote in his two-volume biography of Elvis: "It was like nothing I had ever seen on television before. I don't know if I can convey how truly thrilling a moment it really was."

The reincarnation of Elvis took another turn in January 1969 when he was scheduled to record a new album and some singles for RCA. Elvis had just finished another disheartening movie and was not enthusiastic about the session. RCA decided to use a new studio in Memphis that was run by a man named Chips Moman.

Elvis and Moman hit it off immediately, and for the first time in years, Elvis got excited about making records. One of the songs Moman brought Elvis was a Mac Davis number called "In the Ghetto." It was a "message" song and Elvis, like many singers who didn't want to offend any of their fans, avoided political statements in interviews or his music. Since he had been in the army, for example, Elvis was sometimes asked what he thought about Vietnam War protesters. His usual reply was similar to one he gave in a New York press conference: "I'd just as soon keep my own personal views about that to myself. I'm just an entertainer and I'd rather not say."

But the Mac Davis song touched Elvis deeply, and the more he heard it the more he was determined to do it. The lyrics tell the sad but wrenching story of a boy trapped in the cycle of crime, violence, and even death that youths alienated by poverty confront in a big-city ghetto. The song, which is less than three minutes long, resonates as much today as it did when Elvis first recorded it.

Elvis went through twenty-three takes on one long night and there was again in his voice all the soulful compassion that had been buried under a decade of fame. Elvis spent two weeks in the studio, also recording other songs including "Suspicious Minds," a song about love thwarted by mistrust. When "In the Ghetto" was released, it reached the top ten and gave Elvis his first gold record in four years. "Suspicious Minds" became his first number one single in six years.

Elvis was again riding high. The Colonel signed him for a four-week engagement in Las Vegas at the new International Hotel. For all his trips to Vegas, it would be Elvis's first singing appearance there since he and Scotty and Bill had flopped as a trio.

For the first Vegas show, Elvis put together a new group of musicians. He held auditions in Los Angeles and, to the Colonel's exasperation, spared no expense in getting the players he wanted. He brought in two groups—one black and one white—to sing backup.

Many of the musicians Elvis hired were young players and were not awed by him. Elvis was still Elvis, of course. But by this time he was regarded by many younger musicians as purely retro, a B-movie star who just churned out albums and sound tracks.

But when rehearsals began, Elvis's innate politeness and professionalism made converts out of them all. Many of the musicians had worked with newer pop stars and were used to outbursts of ego from the singers. But Elvis was always patient and encouraging, and by the time the show opened the entire band was behind him.

Elvis just casually strolled onstage without any fanfare, and the room exploded. For the next hour, Elvis gave them all he had. He fed off audiences, and that night he had a feast. Some people said it was a new and different Elvis that night. In fact, it was the old, original Elvis, who gave the performance of a lifetime.

Elvis interspersed the songs with monologues about his life and career. He had them on their feet screaming and he had them in tears. Even the band members were stunned by the performance. In the jargon of the day, Elvis was a happening.

CHAPTER TEN

THE TRIUMPH OF the first Vegas appearance resulted in a contract for Elvis to return for four-week engagements twice a year for the next five years. The one dark cloud hanging over him was the inescapable fact that his marriage was falling apart. After the birth of Lisa Marie, Elvis had refused to have sex with Priscilla and seemed to be avoiding her. If Priscilla was in Los Angeles, Elvis would be in Memphis. If Priscilla came home to Graceland, then Elvis would find a reason to be someplace else.

Then a series of events served to fuel the paranoia that by now was never far from the surface with Elvis. There were several anonymous kidnapping and death threats telephoned to him and his friends. One was so specific about an attempt on his life during one of the Vegas shows, Elvis went onstage with pistols stuck in his boots.

The threats also triggered some strange behavior. Elvis went on a gun-buying spree and once spent twenty thousand dollars in three days buying every kind of firearm he could find. He also embarked on one of the most bizarre escapades of his life.

After an argument with Priscilla and Vernon at Graceland just a few days before Christmas in 1970 that began over money and his obsession with guns, he stormed out of the house. Neither Priscilla nor Vernon took it seriously at first. He had done that before, but he always came back. This time he didn't.

As it turned out, Elvis had flown to Washington, back to Los Angeles, and then returned to Washington again. On the second flight to Washington, Elvis wrote a letter to President Nixon asking for a meeting so they could discuss the drug problem in America. As soon as they landed, Elvis dropped the letter off at the White House gates.

Elvis then went to the Bureau of Narcotics and Dangerous Drugs and tried to convince them to give him a badge as special drug agent, but he was turned down. Then, amazingly, he had a call from the White House saying Nixon would be glad to meet him.

Elvis was dressed more for a Vegas press conference than a meeting with the president of the United States—a purple velvet outfit, a high open-collared white shirt, and a cape. He told Nixon he wanted to help fight the scourge of drugs that was sweeping the country and all he needed was a special agent's badge from the Bureau of Narcotics. He then pulled out all the honorary deputy sheriff's badges he had been given during his career and showed them to Nixon. Beyond all reason, the president agreed to get him a badge as an undercover narc agent.

The final break with Priscilla came in 1972 at the end of one of his Vegas shows. During their frequent separations over the past couple of years, when Priscilla would be in Los Angeles redecorating the house there, Elvis would often fly in a string of different girls to be with him in Memphis. For her part, Priscilla had been seeing a good deal of her karate instructor.

Priscilla had come to Vegas for the opening of the new show, but she had left almost immediately. When she returned at the end of the engagement, she told him she was leaving him. When she left the next morning, she did not tell anyone good-bye.

Within a month, Elvis had a recording session and a tour that included his first ever live appearance in New York City, which sold out four performances. As always, he was the usual witty and charming Elvis in interviews. But it was clear to those close to him that a malaise was once again settling in.

The Colonel finally sealed a deal on a pet project he had been working on—a closed-circuit television special that would be broadcast via satellite for the first time ever around the world. The show was to be staged in Honolulu and called "Aloha From Hawaii." It would be aired the following January and was expected to reach an audience of over one billion people.

With her separation from Elvis now official, Priscilla returned to Graceland in the summer of 1972 to pack all her things. It was also about this time that the thirty-seven-year-old Elvis met a young woman named Linda Thompson, who was the reigning Miss Tennessee. She and Elvis hit it off immediately and he not only invited her back to Graceland but asked her to join him in Vegas for his next appearance there.

The Vegas shows were starting to get a bit rough. Elvis, who once didn't want to hear anyone use profanity around him, was now peppering his monologues with vulgarities. The playful pout that had once been one of his trademarks had turned into a sneering snarl. He was not only overweight but puffy.

When Linda arrived, she noticed that he slurred his words quite a bit, and she even asked him about it. He laughed and explained that it was just the effects of sleeping pills he had to take. Onstage, he more and more frequently forgot the words to songs.

The director NBC had hired for the closed-circuit TV special in Hawaii built a huge stage with a runway jutting out into the audience. The band was on risers behind the stage and the set included a huge sign that spelled out ELVIS with a big flashing image of a man playing guitar as a backdrop.

Elvis had for some time been wearing more flamboyant costumes—gaudy white bell-bottomed jumpsuits with capes and aviator glasses—and in keeping with the grandiosity of his image as the king of rock and roll, as he was now called, the band introduced him by playing the opening bars of Strauss's "Thus Spake

Zarathustra," which had become popular as the theme music to the movie *2001: A Space Odyssey*. It was a circus with Elvis as the ringmaster, lion tamer, high-wire acrobat, and clown all rolled into one.

The show was about as flashy as television could get, and it drew an estimated 1.2 billion viewers around the world, the largest ever at that time. Elvis gave a polished performance, but he never really threw himself into it.

The troubles that began at the last Vegas appearances came out in the open in the months that followed. Elvis had to cancel four performances because of illness at an engagement in Lake Tahoe, Nevada, and he failed even to show up for some of his next recording sessions.

Everyone in the gang, including Vernon and the Colonel, began to focus on the pills Elvis was taking. During the last couple of Vegas shows, Elvis had a string of doctors, including a dentist, in and out of the hotel suite. One of them who flew in from Los Angeles gave Elvis what was described as vitamin injections. In fact, each of the doctors was giving Elvis prescriptions for different drugs.

Everyone, even his father, was afraid to broach the subject with Elvis. When anyone mentioned the amount of pills he was taking, Elvis would insist he was against drugs and would never take any himself. For Elvis, "drugs" were heroin, cocaine, and marijuana. He never seemed to make the connection that what was in his medicine cabinet, which by now was so full of pills it looked like a pharmaceutical warehouse, were also drugs.

Tension between Elvis and the Colonel also had been building on and off for some time over Elvis's spending and his growing dependence on pills and over what Elvis regarded as the Colonel's interference in his private and professional life. The feud came to a head during one Vegas appearance in 1973. In his monologue one night, Elvis took a verbal jab at Conrad Hilton, who had bought the International Hotel. The Colonel was furious and told Elvis not to ever publicly criticize the man who was paying his salary again. Elvis fumed over the Colonel telling him what he could and could not say onstage. He and Parker got into an argument in front of the whole crew. It ended with Elvis shouting, "You're fired," and the Colonel retorting, "You can't fire me, I quit."

The breakup lasted about a week. The Colonel sent Elvis a huge bill for services rendered, but he continued to negotiate on his behalf. But neither the star nor his agent would speak to the other. Just before Elvis was ready to leave at the end of the engagement, he told one of the guys to get Parker on the phone. No one heard the actual conversation, but there were apparently apologies on both sides, and the partnership was patched up.

Elvis's divorce became final in October 9, 1973, under a settlement that granted him visiting rights with Lisa Marie. Three days later he began to have serious problems breathing. He chartered a plane to take him from Los Angeles to Memphis, and Dr. George Nichopoulos, or Dr. Nick as he had come to be known since he treated Elvis on an earlier occasion, came to Graceland immediately. For a couple of days, the doctor tried to treat him at home, but his condition only got worse, and finally the doctor called an ambulance and Elvis was admitted to Baptist Memorial Hospital in Memphis.

A team of doctors examined him, and although he was clearly seriously ill, they could not figure out exactly what was wrong. Dr. Nick asked him about some bruises on his arm and Elvis said they were from acupuncture treatments. The doctor couldn't understand why acupuncture needles would leave bruises, and Elvis explained that the acupuncturist didn't just use needles, but syringes. Asked what was in the syringes, Elvis professed not to know.

Dr. Nick got the "acupuncturist" on the phone, and the California doctor admitted that he had been injecting Elvis with liquid Demerol, a strong brand of sedative and painkiller, on an almost daily basis. Dr. Nick then knew that Elvis would have to be treated as an addict. He started Elvis on methadone, which is often used to wean heroin addicts off the drug, and kept a twenty-four-hour watch on him for withdrawal symptoms. Elvis stayed in the hospital for two weeks, then spent two months recuperating at home.

It was a more subdued Elvis who showed up in Vegas for his next engagement. He had lost some weight in the hospital and looked better than he had for a while. But if anyone thought the episode was going to scare

Elvis into changing his ways for long, he was sadly mistaken. Elvis started a tour immediately after the Vegas shows, and before long he was back using a mix of pills to address his multitude of perceived ailments.

Over the course of the next two years, Elvis slowly dissolved. The Colonel kept organizing tours and recording sessions and dates in Vegas and Tahoe. But Elvis's ability to keep his engagements increasingly became a question mark. He put on so much weight he occasionally would split his pants onstage. But that was the least of the problems. If his behavior had been erratic in the past, it now became almost surreal.

His fascination with guns led him to carry an arsenal of firearms around with him, and he would occasionally shoot out light fixtures or fire through the walls in hotels. Several times he pulled a gun on some member of his entourage who had upset him. Karate and guns were about the only outside interests he had anymore.

Neither his father nor the Colonel had much influence over him. They, too, were having problems. Vernon's marriage to Dee broke up, and he started seeing someone new. The Colonel was a heavy gambler, and he had by now dropped such large amounts of money at the roulette tables he had to keep Elvis working to pay his own debts.

Elvis himself began to throw checks around like they were Monopoly money. He had always been generous, but the spending reached profligate proportions. He gave away cars like they were party favors, sometimes to people he had only just met. He had a jeweler travel with the entourage just so he could buy fine jewelry to give as gifts to hand out on a whim. He began to buy airplanes almost as he had cars when he first came into money.

The bizarre offstage behavior carried over onstage. It was impossible to know what Elvis was going to say or do once he was in front of an audience. He would often ramble incoherently in his monologues. He might recall bitterly some of his early humiliations, like when he had to sing to a dog on the Steve Allen show or when Arthur Godfrey wouldn't even listen to him, or when he was told by a honky-tonk owner he should stick to driving a truck.

Some of his comments were vicious and would be directed at members of the band or the backup groups, or even his girlfriends. One after another musician or singer walked out, and it was getting to be a problem finding replacements in the middle of a tour or an engagement.

The string of girlfriends was another problem. By this time, Elvis could not bear to be alone, even while he slept. Linda was his most constant companion, but every time he saw someone new who struck his fancy, he would pack Linda off and concentrate on the new girl.

Shortly after his fortieth birthday in 1975, Elvis was hospitalized again. Linda had awoken in the night to find him struggling for breath. While Elvis was in the hospital, Vernon suffered a heart attack, and Elvis and his father ended up sharing a room.

Seven months later, as he was on his way to a Vegas engagement, his plane had to make an emergency landing in Dallas because he was short of breath. After resting for a few hours, he flew on to Vegas and the show went on. On the second night, however, he lay down on the stage at one point. By the fourth night, the entire engagement was canceled and Elvis was flown home to Memphis.

Once again, Elvis went back into the hospital. But no one was under any illusions that this time would be any different from previous hospital stays. Despite all his anti-drug statements, Elvis had added cocaine to his diet of medications, which now also included Dilaudid, a powerful painkiller that was usually prescribed for cancer patients.

Elvis spent two weeks in the hospital, then a long recuperation at Graceland. The Colonel finally booked him into another engagement in Vegas for December, and a New Year's Eve concert in Pontiac, Michigan. Elvis was nervous about returning to Vegas and had never played a New Year's Eve concert before. But he needed the money.

He was by now nearly broke. He had not worked in almost four months, since the canceled Vegas shows in August, and hundreds of thousands of dollars in bills were coming in for the airplanes, cars, jewelry, guns, and clothes that he had been buying. He even took out a loan on Graceland to help pay his debts. Vernon and the Colonel persuaded him that he also had to cut his staff payroll, and Elvis finally agreed.

At the end of a summer tour in 1976, Vernon called Red West and his cousin, Sonny West, two of Elvis's closest aides, and told them they were fired. For Red, who had been defending Elvis ever since he tried out for the football team at Humes High School, it was like a stab in the back that Elvis himself couldn't have made the call.

For the next year, Elvis just went through the motions. The Colonel would schedule recording dates, but Elvis showed up for only some of the sessions. He continued to make appearances at Tahoe and Vegas, and he went out on tours, but he was even more unpredictable onstage, and they all considered it a success if he just got through a show without collapsing or walking off. Everyone tiptoed around him. He was like a caged tiger that everyone was afraid to get too near lest he bite them.

Girlfriends came and went on a whim, and in the fall he met a new one, Ginger Alden, who was not all that impressed by his usual line, and who refused to move into Graceland. Possibly it was her ambivalence that challenged him, but she quickly became his favorite and he even proposed two months after meeting her.

As if his own condition wasn't enough to deal with, Elvis was hit with a barrage of other problems. He heard that Red West was writing a tell-all book about his years with Elvis, there were stories in the newspapers that Colonel Parker was trying to sell his contract, and Vernon had been hospitalized a second time for a suspected heart attack.

Still he went out. In June 1977 he left for his fifth tour of the year, one that was going to be filmed by CBS for a TV special, and another was scheduled for August. In between, Lisa Marie came from California for a two-week visit at the end of July.

Elvis bought his nine-year-old daughter a pony and one night he rented the old Memphis Fairgrounds, now a theme park called Libertyland, for a special party for Lisa Marie. He even rode some of the rides himself.

A week later, Lisa Marie was getting ready to return to Priscilla in California, and Elvis was preparing to leave the following night for the tour. For years now, Elvis had lived as though night were day and day were night, and anyone who worked for him simply adjusted their watches to Elvis's time zone.

Ginger was going to spend the night, and she went with him to a ten thirty P.M. dentist appointment. After getting his teeth cleaned and a cavity filled, he asked for and received some codeine tablets in case he got a toothache. He got home a little after midnight.

Shortly after two A.M. he called Dr. Nick and told him a tooth he had just had filled was hurting him and asked him for some Dilaudid. The doctor phoned in a prescription to an all-night pharmacy, and Elvis sent someone to pick it up. Two hours later he called his cousin Billy Smith, who was now living with his wife Jo on the Graceland grounds.

Elvis asked Billy if he would like to play some racquetball, and although it was the middle of the night and they had been asleep and it was raining, Billy and Jo got dressed and went over to the racquetball courts to join Elvis and Ginger. They knocked the ball around a bit, then Elvis got tired and sat down at the piano and began to play Willie Nelson's song "Blue Eyes Cryin' in the Rain." When they got back to the house, Billy washed Elvis's hair and left.

Elvis took one of the packets of drugs that Dr. Nick had concocted to help him get to sleep. Each one contained a cocktail of Seconal, Placidyl, Valmid, Tuinal, Demerol, and other drugs. Elvis was still awake a couple of hours later and took a second packet. He still couldn't get to sleep, and around noon he took a third packet of the drugs and told Ginger he was going to the bathroom. Ginger went to sleep.

She awoke around one thirty in the afternoon and

called her mother. Her mother asked how Elvis was and Ginger said she didn't know. He had gone to the bathroom but hadn't returned. Maybe she should check.

Elvis was lying facedown in a pool of vomit. Ginger called downstairs for help. Al Strada, Elvis's personal valet, was the first to arrive, and he was followed almost immediately by Joe Esposito, an old army buddy of Elvis's who had been part of the gang since Germany and who had just arrived that day from California. Joe managed to turn him over and tried to give him mouth-to-mouth resuscitation.

Within minutes the general alarm had gone out. Vernon arrived and kept saying over and over, "Oh, God, son, please don't die." But it was clear to anyone standing there that it was already over. Elvis's face was swollen and purple, his tongue was sticking out of his mouth and turning black, and his eyes were red.

Suddenly Lisa Marie arrived screaming, "What's wrong with my daddy?" Ginger closed the bathroom door so she couldn't see.

Two firemen and an ambulance arrived within minutes. They found no vital signs, but they put Elvis on a stretcher and carried him to the ambulance. Dr. Nick arrived about the same time and got into the back, trying to revive him as they drove to the hospital and shouting, "Breathe, Elvis, breathe for me."

They carried him into an emergency room, and a team of doctors worked for half an hour before giving up. It was August 16, 1977, and Elvis Aron Presley was forty-two years old. An autopsy was performed, but the doctors listed the cause of death as "cardiac arrhythmia due to undetermined heartbeat." It was medical mumbo jumbo, and the final lab report said fourteen different drugs were found in his system.

Vernon insisted that the funeral be held at Graceland and that there be a public viewing of the body the day before. A crowd estimated at fifty thousand people lined up on the street outside Graceland before the big gates swung open to allow people to walk by the copper-lined casket four abreast. The lawn outside the mansion was a carpet of flowers, and it took a fleet of vans four hours to transport them all to the cemetery.

The service itself was dominated by music. Several of the gospel singers and groups that had inspired Elvis as a youth performed, including James Blackwood, who had sung at Gladys's funeral and who sang at Elvis's one of his favorite hymns, "How Great Thou

Art." C. W. Bradley, a Church of Christ minister of the congregation Vernon's ex-wife Dee attended, preached the sermon.

The cortege to the cemetery consisted of forty nine cars in addition to the hearse, and a crowd of between fifteen thousand and twenty thousand people lined the road to wave a last good-bye. Vernon was the last to leave, and he had to be helped back to the car. The funeral party returned to Graceland for what was described as a Southern supper, and Vernon sent word that all the floral wreaths should be broken up and a flower given to each of the fans who were already keeping vigil at the cemetery.

There have been a plethora of eulogies and apologies over Elvis in the years since his death, and there is no need for another one. Beyond all the impersonators and the kitschy memorabilia that have turned him into a cult, the true influence Elvis had on our music and culture will be decided only by time. I remember feeling very sad when I learned of his death. By that time my own music tastes had moved on. But among my souvenirs, I still have two Sun Records 78s, and I will never part with them, although it's almost impossible find a phonograph to play them on. Hearing the early songs like "Good Rockin' Tonight" or "Mystery Train" can still transport me back to the exuberance of my own youth and rekindle the rebel spirit that represents the best of rock and roll.

For cultural historians, Elvis was a jumble of contradictions that reflected the times in which he lived, and there is heated debate over which Elvis was the "real" Elvis. For me he will always remain—despite the aberrations of behavior induced by all the drugs—the polite young man who was shy and insecure, who said "ma'am" and "sir" and tried to answer all questions as truthfully as he could, who loved music and wanted only to sing, who was grateful to those who would listen, and who would stand for hours signing autographs in the driveway of his home. I think Dixie Locke probably saw the real Elvis more clearly than anyone when she said he just wanted to please people. And to that end, his life's dream came true.

In the finale of his spectacular 1968 Comeback Special, Elvis poured his heart and soul into performing "If I Can Dream."

SOURCE NOTES

FOREWORD

"Before there was . . .": Quoted in Chadwick, *In Search of Elvis*, 21.

INTRODUCTION

"You know, what . . ." to "Girls, I'll see you backstage": Interview with Mae Boren Axton, Guralnick, *Last Train*, pp. 186–90.

CHAPTER ONE

Sings with church choir, age 2: *TV Radio Mirror* editors, *Elvis Presley*, 8, cited in Guralnick, *Last Train*, 14.

"Don't you worry . . .": Lopert, "The Boy with the Big Beat," quoted in Guralnick, *Last Train*, 15.

"We were broke . . .": Kingsley, "At Home with Elvis," quoted in Guralnick, *Last Train*, 28.

"Poor we were . . .": Anderson, "Elvis by His Father," quoted in Guralnick, *Last Train*, 29.

CHAPTER TWO

"He had a little . . .": Guralnick, *Last Train*, 40.

"felt sorry for him": West, *Elvis: What Happened?*, 17.

"had established a reputation . . .": Porteous, "Prison Singers May Find Fame," quoted in Guralnick, *Last Train*, 57.

"What kind of singer . . . nobody": Guralnick, *Last Train*, 63.

"sounded like somebody . . ." "interesting" and "good ballad singer . . .": Guralnick, *Last Train*, 64.

CHAPTER THREE

Dixie Locke meeting Elvis: Guralnick, *Last Train*, 68–69.

"I was there . . .": Guralnick, *Last Train*, 84.

"What do you want . . .": Guralnick, *Last Train*, 93.

"What are you . . . do it again": Guralnick, *Last Train*, 95.

"hearing them say . . .": Dundy, *Elvis and Gladys*, 180–81.

"I played that record . . .": Leonard, "Elvis Presley: The New Singing Rage," 13.

"I was scared . . ." and "Aren't you going . . . the whole time": Guralnick, *Last Train*, 101.

CHAPTER FOUR

"Hurry Home . . .": Guralnick, *Last Train*, 105.

"Everybody was hollering . . ." and "The more I did . . .": Paul Wilder interview quoted in Guralnick, *Last Train*, 110.

CHAPTER FIVE

"Just keep what . . ." and "What did I do? . . .": Guralnick, *Last Train*, 133.

"Mr. Atkins, my guitar . . .": Guralnick, *Last Train*, 128.

"this boy is . . .": Guralnick, *Last Train*, 129.

"Man, have you ever . . .": Guralnick, *Last Train*, 141.

"You should make . . .": Osborne, *Elvis: Word for Word*, 246.

"Shucks, it still played . . .": Johnson, *Elvis Presley Speaks!*, 16.

"dollar marks in . . .": Guralnick, *Last Train*, 190.

"to negotiate all . . .": quoted in Guralnick, *Last Train*, 210.

CHAPTER SIX

"Hot dog, play . . .": Guralnick, *Last Train*, 229.

"Honey, that may work . . ." and "We've found the . . .": Guralnick, *Last Train*, 242.

"a young fellow . . .": Guralnick, *Last Train*, 210.

"electricity bounced off . . ." and "amateurish conviction": Guralnick, *Last Train*, 260.

"I owe it all . . .": Guralnick, *Last Train*, 263.

"How about my boy?": Guralnick, *Last Train*, 283.

"achieved a new . . .": Guralnick, *Last Train*, 321.

"Well . . . those people . . ." to ". . . best that I can": Guralnick, *Last Train*, 296.

"two thousand idiots": Herbert Rau in *Miami News*, quoted in Guralnick, *Last Train*, 319.

"Sir, those kids . . .": Guralnick, *Last Train*, 319–20.

CHAPTER SEVEN

"I used to sing . . .": Guralnick, *Last Train*, 329.

"Tupelo Welcomes Elvis . . .": Guralnick, *Last Train*, 340.

"It made me feel . . .": Dundy, *Elvis and Gladys*, 260.

"I wanted to say . . .": Guralnick, *Last Train*, 379.

"There's somebody to comb . . .": Jennings, "There'll Always Be an Elvis," 79.

CHAPTER EIGHT

"If I seem . . .": Guralnick, *Last Train*, 461.

"Hair today . . .": Guralnick, *Last Train*, 463.

"I knew what it was . . .": Guralnick, *Last Train*, 474.

"Look, Dad, here's Dixie" to ". . . too far to get out": Guralnick, *Last Train*, 477–79.

Sergeant gives Elvis amphetamines: West, *Elvis: What Happened?*, 186.

"Hi, I'm Elvis . . ." to "Ninth . . . Grade": Presley, *Elvis and Me*, 28.

"Well, sir, I happen . . .": Guralnick, *Careless Love*, 41.

"The Girl He Left Behind": Caption in "Farewell to Priscilla," 97.

"He is my father . . .": *Memphis Press-Scimitar,* July 7, 1960, quoted in Guralnick, *Careless Love*, 78.

Priscilla visits Elvis in Los Angeles: Presley, *Elvis and Me*, 69–74.

CHAPTER NINE

"For the first year . . .": Presley, *Elvis and Me*, 248.

"She's a little . . .": Guralnick, *Careless Love*, 289.

"No, I like . . ." and "Do what you . . .": Guralnick, *Careless Love*, 297.

Elvis plays "Moonlight Sonata": Guralnick, *Careless Love*, 303.

"I want to tour . . .": Guralnick, *Careless Love*, 317.

"It was like nothing . . .": Guralnick, *Careless Love*, 323.

"I'd just as soon . . .": Osborne, *Word for Word*, 257.

CHAPTER TEN

Argument with Priscilla and Vernon: Presley, *Elvis and Me*, 285.

"You're fired" and "You can't fire me, I quit.": Guralnick, *Careless Love*, 506.

Plane makes emergency landing: West, *Elvis: What Happened?*, 198.

"Oh, God, son . . ." to ". . . undetermined heartbeat": Guralnick, *Careless Love*, 647–51.

BIBLIOGRAPHY

Anderson, Nancy. "Elvis by His Father Vernon Presley." *Good Houskeeping*, January 1978.

Booth, Stanley. "A Hound Dog to the Manor Born." *Esquire*, February 1968.

Burk, Bill E. *Early Elvis: The Humes Years*. Memphis: Red Oak Press, 1990.

Chadwick, Vernon, editor. *In Search of Elvis: Music, Race, Art, Religion*. Boulder, Colo.: Westview Press, 1997.

Dundy, Elaine. *Elvis and Gladys*. New York: Macmillan, 1985.

Elvis: '68 Comeback (DVD). BMG Heritage, 2006.

"Farewell to Priscilla, Hello U.S.A.: Sergeant Elvis Comes Back Home to the Girls He Left Behind." *LIFE*, March 14, 1960.

Goldman, Albert. *Elvis*. New York: McGraw-Hill, 1981.

Guralnick, Peter. *Careless Love: The Unmaking of Elvis Presley*. Boston: Back Bay Books/Little, Brown and Company, 1999.

———. *Last Train to Memphis: The Rise of Elvis Presley*. Boston: Back Bay Books/Little, Brown and Company, 1994.

Jennings, C. Robert. "There'll Always Be an Elvis." *Saturday Evening Post*, September 11, 1965.

Johnson, Robert. *Elvis Presley Speaks!* New York: Rave Publishing, 1956.

Kingsley, James. "At Home with Elvis Presley." *Memphis Commercial Appeal, Mid-South Magazine*, March 7, 1956.

Leonard, Elston. "Elvis Presley: The New Singing Rage." *Tiger*, circa 1956.

Lopert, Martha. "The Boy with the Big Beat." *Celebrity*, Winter 1958.

Memphis Commercial Appeal. Interview with Elvis Presley. September 29, 1968.

Osborne, Jerry. *Elvis: Word for Word*. New York: Gramercy Books/Random House, Inc., 2006.

Porteous, Clark. "Prison Singers May Find Fame with Record They Made in Memphis." *Memphis Press-Scimitar*, July 15, 1953.

Presley, Priscilla Beaulieu, with Sandra Harmon. *Elvis and Me*. New York: Berkley Books/Penguin Putnam, 1986.

TV Radio Mirror editors. *Elvis Presley*. New York: Bartholemew House, 1956.

West, Red, Sonny West, and Dave Hebler, as told to Steve Dunleavy. *Elvis: What Happened?* New York: Ballantine Books, 1977.

INDEX

PHOTO CREDITS

Page 16: MichaelOchsArchives.com

Page 27: Elvis image used by permission, © Elvis Presley Enterprises, Inc.

Pages 32: Elvis image used by permission, © Elvis Presley Enterprises, Inc.

Page 48: MichaelOchsArchives.com

Page 61: Elvis image used by permission, © Elvis Presley Enterprises, Inc.

Page 81: MichaelOchsArchives.com

Page 90: Elvis image used by permission, © Elvis Presley Enterprises, Inc.

Page 112: Elvis image used by permission, © Elvis Presley Enterprises, Inc.

Page 131: Elvis image used by permission, © Elvis Presley Enterprises, Inc.

Page 151: Elvis image used by permission, © Elvis Presley Enterprises, Inc.

Page 179: Elvis image used by permission, © Elvis Presley Enterprises, Inc.

ACKNOWLEDGMENTS

FIRST OF ALL, I would like to thank Jill Davis for asking me to be a part of this project. I especially want to express my gratitude to Anne Gunton, whose enthusiasm and expert editorial advice was invaluable and provided a great source of strength. Janet Pascal's meticulous and exhaustive attention to the smallest details was an immense help, and Jim Hoover brought it all into focus with his exciting designs. The encouragement of Mary Osborne and Mickey and Alan Friedman sustained me throughout the writing of the book. It would be remiss of me not to mention the countless writers and photographers who chronicled the life of Elvis Aron Presley, especially Peter Guralnick, whose definitive two-volume account of his remarkable life is a model of the biographer's art. Finally, as in all good things in my life, this book is a reflection of the inspiration of my wife, LuAnn Walther.